# COMMUNES IN AMERICA
# The Place Just Right

# COMMUNES IN AMERICA
# The Place Just Right
by Elinor Lander Horwitz

J. B. LIPPINCOTT COMPANY
PHILADELPHIA AND NEW YORK

U.S. Library of Congress Cataloging in Publication Data

Horwitz, Elinor Lander.
  Communes in America.

  SUMMARY: Traces the history of collective settlements in the
United States and compares their organization and purpose with the
communes of today.
  1. Collective settlements—United States—History—Juvenile literature. 2. United States—Social conditions—1960–    —Juvenile literature. [1. Collective settlements—United States—History] I. Title.
HX654.H58      335'.02'0973      72-3685
ISBN-0-397-31437-X

FOR

GERTRUDE AND HARRY

# Contents

COMMUNES IN AMERICA
# The Place Just Right

'TIS THE GIFT TO BE SIMPLE, 'TIS THE GIFT TO BE FREE,

'TIS THE GIFT TO COME DOWN WHERE WE OUGHT TO BE.

AND WHEN WE FIND OURSELVES IN THE PLACE JUST RIGHT,

'TWILL BE IN THE VALLEY OF LOVE AND DELIGHT.

—FROM A SHAKER SONG, "SIMPLE GIFTS"

# 1 ALL THINGS COMMON

ONE OF THE MOST universal and persistent ideals men have cherished through the ages is that of a perfect society. Defining and describing utopias has long been a favorite activity of fiction writers, philosophers, statesmen, and city planners. Through the ages, utopian ideals have stimulated social change, economic reform, and—in some periods —violent revolution. One of the most fascinating results of man's enduring faith that an ideal society can be *attained* as well as imagined has been a rich and bizarre history of planned experimental communities in which men and women have turned theory into action by dropping out of an imperfect world to live life, not as it *is*—but as they feel it should be.

Most people look on today's rural communes as a radically original invention of the city-weary hippies of the sixties, rather than as a revival of an alternate life-style with a history that spans the development of this country. The communal movement, which began in America in pre-Revolutionary days, spread and flowered in the nineteenth century, when literally hundreds of planned communities attracted men and women of a vast range of social and religious beliefs. What we now call a "commune," and what sociologists refer to as an "intentional community," was known in the last century as a "community," a "collective," a "family," an "association." Today's communitarians, most of them totally unaware of their historical counterparts, have used all these terms and given them precisely the same definition: a group of people who have come together voluntarily to live by brotherly cooperation and sharing in a microsociety of their own making.

Many of the nineteenth-century communitarians were inspired by convictions which still sound extraordinarily daring today. Furthermore, they practiced what they preached despite persecutions in an age when rigid rules of conformity turned violators into permanent social outcasts. Like today's communitarians they believed that society had gone astray in worshipping the false gods of competition and financial prosperity. They believed almost mystically in the value of returning to the land. They denied the value of material possessions and the necessity for employer, landlord, middleman, or a standardized work week. They believed in the nobility of common labor and the practice of simple crafts. They also preached abolition, promoted racial and sexual equality, and tried out new forms of education.

With the notable exception of Brook Farm—which in many other ways seems the most "modern" of nineteenth-century communes—the old communities denied traditional views of sex, marriage, and child rearing. In some of these "families" the central concept of sharing was interpreted to literally include the self, and the term "free-love association" announced to the world the community's attitude on *that* issue. It was commonly believed that the "selfish" and "possessive" relationship between one man and one woman was repugnant to the spirit of community. One commune of the 1820s promoted interracial free love. In groups such as the Shakers and the Rappites, the rule was celibacy—total avoidance of sexual relations and marriage. The Oneida Community worked out a unique set of principles which combined free love, birth control, and eugenics—the then unnamed science of producing desired hereditary characteristics in the next generation through selective mating. Children were often reared communally as the love objects and responsibility of all the members. On the better-organized communes they were likely to be housed together apart from their parents in a nursery or children's house, as on today's Israeli kibbutzim. They were cared for and educated by members of the community, and their liberated mothers worked in the fields with the men.

Nineteenth-century communitarians often flaunted conventional fashion in dress with as much rebellious determination as any twentieth-century hippie. The Shakers and

Rappites wore extremely simple and modest habits; the ladies of Oneida cut their skirts short—the better to work in; the cultured and educated Brook Farmers affected rustic peasant shirts. Men on communes grew beards when they went out of style in the cities, and women let their hair hang loose or sheared it off at the ears as a symbol of emancipation in a period when all "decent" women were coiling their long tresses into buns and chignons.

All sorts of food fads were practiced with spiritual earnestness on the old communes, and special meals were usually available for people who would eat only bread made with unprocessed flour and other natural foods. Vegetarianism was popular, meat-eating being considered a detriment to health and to spirituality, and the shameful evidence of man's inhumanity to beasts. Religious mysticism flourished during the mid-nineteenth century; refusal to serve in the armed forces had the status of a creed; nudism was a respected conviction.

What sort of people lived on these nineteenth-century communes? Or, for that matter, what sort of people are attracted to communal life now? Here again the parallels are striking. There were then, and there are today, committed idealistic people who sincerely believe in communal life and in its possibilities for joy and self-enrichment. They want to simplify life, to cast off possessions. "Most of the luxuries, and many of the so-called comforts of life are not only not indispensable, but positive hindrances to the elevation of mankind," wrote Henry David Thoreau, who returned to nature in solitude at Walden Pond in 1854.

But idealists are by no means the only people who form or live on communes. A look at today's experiments and a look into the past both reveal that communes have always attracted kooks, freaks, lawbreakers, the immature, the irresponsible, and a limitless variety of dissatisfied and frustrated misfits. Many people in the old communities simply drifted from one commune to another as a way of life, and their spiritual descendants are drifting through communities in California and New Mexico today. Horace Greeley, who was enthusiastic about associations, wrote that it was these destructive oddballs who wrecked communities which might otherwise have succeeded. The Shakers were so familiar with the problem of out-and-out freeloaders that they termed "Winter Shakers" the hordes of men and women who would arrive when the harvest was over, mouth pious sentiments, sit before the fire, and eat heartily all winter—and disappear on the first spring day suitable for plowing.

Many early communes were formed by immigrants from Europe, to whom America loomed as the land where social, moral, and economic reforms could be effected without violence and bloodshed—where the tyranny of class and tradition could be left behind forever. The entire country seemed a utopia to the persecuted, the disillusioned —and to many of the intellectual young. Samuel Taylor Coleridge tried to induce a group of poets to join him in founding a commune in Virginia. He idolized George Washington and Thomas Paine and was inspired by the vision of the American democracy where Europeans could escape the despotism of monarchs. The Icarians were utopian thinkers, disillusioned by the failure of the French Revolution, who thought that an ideal society could be established in Texas—the newest state in the new land of freedom.

The early communes are easily divided into religious and nonreligious communities. A similar division is possible today, although the do-your-own-thing philosophy can result in an association of people of widely different beliefs. The more durable contemporary communes, however, still seem to be those in which there are enough common ideals—religious or simply human—to enable members to overcome the inevitable problems of living together. As a woman who tried it for two years explains, "A commune just isn't going to continue to exist without a goal. When the going gets rough you have to have a really strong reason to stick together." A nineteenth-century commentator who visited many associations made the same observation. "To insure strength and success," he said, "a community must be either religious in its focus or be made up of people with enough shared beliefs to take the place of a religion."

In a religious commune—whether the faith be German sectarian Protestantism, spiritualism, or Zen Buddhism —members regard themselves as having fled a corrupt world to live their beliefs in peace. They are usually guided by a leader, high priest, or guru, who may be considered an actual deity or simply a person of particular wisdom or inspiration. Obedience, humility, and order are glorified in religious communities, whereas individuality is cherished in secular communities. What a religious community offers is salvation, whereas a secular community aims—primarily —toward happiness through attainment of "the good life."

Historically, the religious communes have survived longest in this country. The Shakers came from England before the Revolution and a handful are still alive today. The other longevity records were set by German religious communities: the Ephratans—205 years; the Rappites —a century; the Zoarites—83 years; the Amanans— 87. The Hutterites, who came in 1874 with 400 members, now have 13,000 living in 115 colonies in the United States and Canada. The members of the Society of Brothers, who fled Nazi Germany in 1935, have three thriving communities in New York, Pennsylvania, and Connecticut.

Some religious groups dropped communal living early in their history. The Mormons, after eighteen months of community, abandoned the practice in favor of tithing— donating one-tenth of each year's income to the group. Other religious communes were short-lived and obscure, and their far-out beliefs repelled possible converts. One nineteenth-century group in upstate New York interpreted the biblical injunction to let the dead bury their dead as meaning that the living had no right to do so. They created a public nuisance after accumulating a number of decaying corpses.

Why do the majority of communes collapse so quickly? Brook Farm, the most idealistic and best-known of the secular communes, where Nathaniel Hawthorne and other leading intellectuals pitched manure and milked cows, survived only six years. The farm—which was intended to serve as a model to the world of a life based on simple humane values—failed for complex economic reasons, a major single cause for the breakup of many communes today. Lack of strong leadership is another common source of failure. Many communes flounder when a particularly magnetic founder leaves or dies. The outrage of neighbors closed down a number of communes in the early history of the movement, and the end of the Land of Oz, a commune which survived less than six months on a farm in Meadville, Pennsylvania, is a recent example of the same process. Internal battles tormented the nineteenth-century Icarian communities, and many people of goodwill on today's communes simply find brotherhood, sisterhood, loving cooperation, and compromise easier to believe in than to live with. "Intentional families" have broken up in battles about how the money should be spent or who is to wash the dishes.

Many older communes bore the seeds of their extinction within their philosophy. Both the Shakers and the Rappites successfully preached celibacy and failed to produce a second generation. The Shakers were highly successful at attracting converts until the period of the Civil War, when communal living lost popularity. They adopted orphans, but the majority drifted off to the outside world in adulthood. The Rappites and many other German religious communes depended on new arrivals from the old country, but the wave of immigration tapered off.

There are estimated to be nearly two thousand urban and rural communes today in thirty-four states. The writer Robert Houriet, who covered ten thousand miles visiting communes all over the country, reported that none was economically self-sufficient. Nonetheless, many people regard communal living as an alternate life-style that will be a major social force in the seventies.

Many of the new communitarians and a majority of the old have been inspired by the description of the lives of the early Christians in the Book of Acts, who held "all things common; and sold their possessions and goods, and parted them to all men, as every man had need."

And yet, despite the fact that community as a way of life has a long and rather colorful history, most of its advocates have sensed that this was something new, daring, and utterly unique. Nathaniel Hawthorne wrote of his arrival at Brook Farm in 1841, "We had left the rusty iron frame-work of society behind us; we had broken through many hindrances that are powerful enough to keep most people on the weary treadmill of the established system." Hawthorne, like many present communitarians, eventually lost his enthusiasm for communal living. He felt oppressed by lack of privacy and he developed an inappropriate disdain for cleaning stables and feeding pigs. He returned to the outside world, but years later he tried to unravel what went wrong. He wrote, with a wistful and poetic sense of missed opportunities, "We had struck upon what ought to be a truth. Posterity may dig it up and profit by it."

# 2 LITERARY UTOPIAS

WHERE IS UTOPIA?

Literally, *utopia* means "nowhere" from the Greek words ου τοπος ("no place"). The word has come to mean "ideal place" because of a book written in the sixteenth century by that man of all seasons, Sir Thomas More. To the intellectuals of More's day the idea of naming an imaginary land with a model society "the island of Nowhere" must have seemed a superbly cynical witticism, since the book not only represented More's vision of a perfect social order but, by implication, formed a vivid criticism of the very imperfect legal and social institutions of More's homeland, the island of Britain. Two authors of famous nineteenth-century utopian novels also enjoyed play-

ing with the true meaning of the word: Samuel Butler with
the title *Erewhon* (try reading it backwards) and William
Morris, who named his book *News From Nowhere.*

Many of the people who have started experimental communities have been inspired by utopian tales written in
classical Greece, Renaissance England, eighteenth-century
France, twentieth-century America. Of course, utopian
thinking is not confined to novelists and philosophers. The
Declaration of Independence is a utopian document written by men who were seeking to establish the framework
for an ideal social order in America. Utopian thinking—
the hope for a better world—led to the French Revolution
in 1789 and the Russian Revolution in 1917.

On the less lofty level, the dream of an ideal land seeps
into virtually everyone's wishful thinking, and "utopia"
implies escape from the real world rather than a plan for
reform of society. Utopia becomes the Garden of Eden,
Robinson Crusoe's island, the land of milk and honey, the
lost continent of Atlantis, Xanadu, the land where the
bong tree grows. Or how about the spiritual utopias promised after life: the Happy Hunting Grounds of the Indians,
the Heaven of Christianity? The painter Paul Gaugin
made a visual utopia of Tahiti, and many people who have
never left home feel quite the same way about other tropical islands such as Bali, Samoa, Hawaii. Islands—because
of their inaccessibility—and gardens—because of their
beauty—have always seemed particularly apt locations
for Utopia. In the infertile biblical lands the paradise God
created east of Eden was inevitably described as tropical
and lush. The word *paradise* is, in Greek, the word for
"garden."

Curiously, the novelist James Hilton located Utopia in Shangri-La in his book *Lost Horizons*. Shangri-La, situated in Tibet, was considerably chillier than is proper for a utopia, and perhaps only in the stark Depression years when the book was written could that forbidding land sound inviting. It did, however, offer the necessary romantic remoteness and it also had another particularly alluring utopian feature, which was that no one ever grew old in Shangri-La. Apparently, that compensated for the climate.

Before turning to the story of actual utopian experiments in this country, it's interesting to see how many of the ideals associated with planned communities appear in the great classics of utopian literature. The two most famous and influential of these are Plato's *Republic*, written in the fourth century B.C., and Sir Thomas More's *Utopia*, written in sixteenth-century England. Both deal with universal social issues: poverty and wealth, property and labor, marriage and the family, education—and such basic needs as clothing, shelter, food. The *Republic* is a blueprint for an ideal commonwealth, whereas More's work is set forth as a tale told by a sailor about an island he visited during a voyage of exploration. Both societies—the Republic and Utopia—are based on a simple agricultural economy.

Plato was twenty-three years old when his city, Athens, was defeated by Sparta in the Peloponnesian War. The *Republic* reflects the young aristocrat's admiration of the more highly structured city of Sparta and his disillusionment with the individualism and liberalism of Athens. Plato's proposed state is an aristocracy of the intellect. It is a land without wealth or poverty in which men live together, helping each other and finding happiness by fulfilling the duties for which each is particularly qualified. He divides the citizens into three classes: the guardians, the soldiers, and the common men. Only the guardians, chosen for their superior abilities, have political power. Membership in a class is hereditary, although a young man or woman of extraordinary ability or remarkable ineptitude may be upgraded or demoted in rank.

Plato contends that a woman is no different from a man in her natural talents or educational requirements, and then he dilutes this remarkably modern point of view a bit by pointing out how gifted women are in weaving and making pancakes! Nonetheless, he decrees that in the Republic women shall be educated along with men in all subjects, including physical culture. He realizes that people will be amused at first to see men and women exercising together naked in the gymnasium in the Greek manner, but he predicts that the sight will become commonplace in time. Women who display superior qualities are to be selected as wives for the guardians, but all wives and all children born to them will be common.

The legislator will study his people, much as a farmer would his animals, and select those most fit to produce the next generation. At certain festivals, lots will be drawn which will designate the men and women to be paired for the purpose of producing offspring, but the legislator will have tampered with the lots in advance to be certain that everything works according to plan! Children will be taken from their mothers immediately after birth and reared together by nurses in a separate building. All care will be taken to see that no mother knows her own child or vice versa.

Plato was interested in genetics over two thousand years before Gregor Mendel experimented with hereditary characteristics. He was also concerned with population control, and he specified exact ages during which people would be allowed to reproduce to avoid overpopulation.

Plato has been widely criticized for his views on artistic censorship. He was deeply aware of the power of great art to sway minds and passions, and he decreed that in the Republic only that music, art, drama, and poetry which directly served the interests of the state was to be permitted. Vigilant censorship of all the arts was to be the guiding law.

The educational system was carefully structured. From ages three to six, children were to learn religious and moral truths by means of carefully screened myths and fables. From ages seven to ten, their physical fitness was to be built up in the gymnasium. Between the tenth and thirteenth years boys and girls were to study reading and writing. From thirteen to fifteen, music and poetry, also carefully censored, were the curriculum. Mathematics and science would be taught to sixteen- to eighteen-year-olds, and at this point, the warrior class was to leave school and concentrate on the arts of war. The guardians, however, were to study until they were thirty. From the age of thirty until they reached fifty they would serve in various governmental posts, taking turns in the role of leader or legislator. Retirement to a life of philosophic study began at fifty.

More's *Utopia* was also written in an era of discord and violence. His dismay at the sufferings of the poor in sixteenth-century England led him to begin his book by plunging directly into an attack on the custom of hanging men for minor offenses, particularly theft. This great humanist clearly saw the relationship of poverty and crime. Like Plato, he set forth a commonwealth in which there would be neither poor nor rich, in which all goods would be held in common. He specifically credits Plato with the idea of abolition of private property. However, unlike Plato's Republic, More's Utopia is a totally classless society.

More had lived through the discovery of America, which gave great impetus to utopian imaginings. There was, of course, enormous excitement all over Europe about current explorations in the Western Hemisphere. More's tale is related by a Portuguese sailor with the unlikely name of Raphael Hythlodaeus, who has just returned from five happy years on the island of Utopia. He tells his story in an English garden. The island of Utopia, he says, has fifty-four towns, all of which are built on the same plan. One of these is the capital, to which each city sends three elected officials as its representatives. All houses are identical and, in order to avoid developing a selfish attachment to property, the people switch homes every ten years. There are no locks on any door and, since all property is communal, any Utopian can walk into any house on the island whenever he wishes. People in Utopia live in families, but a maximum number of people per family is set, and those who overproduce simply pass on the extra children to a less fruitful couple.

Raphael explains that in the system of complete equality

which exists in Utopia, each person learns to farm, and each also learns a useful trade. The farms are outside the cities and men and women live and work on them in rotation. Another mark of equality is that all women dress precisely alike and so do all men, and there is never any change of fashion whatsoever. In Utopia women work equally with men and—here More takes a sharp look at England—there are no idle females or noblemen or clergymen.

Because the labor is shared, only six daily work hours are required of each citizen to keep everyone well provided with all necessities. No one, he points out, toils all day to keep others in unnecessary luxuries. The result is that sometimes a surplus of goods and crops occurs and then the work day is temporarily cut even shorter.

The book is permeated with More's intense desire to right social wrongs by freeing the poor from brutalizing hardships and injustices. He wants leisure and the good life for all—enriched by enjoyments such as reading, recreational games, music, and good food. His Utopians rise early for educational lectures, and people who show extraordinary intelligence are excused throughout life from labor so that they may devote themselves to study. It is, of course, vital that no one learn to love luxury and since diamonds, pearls, and rubies are found on the cliffs of Utopia, people string them as ornaments for infants. The babies look charming and enjoy the pretty jewels, but as they grow older and realize that adults do not wear such gaudy adornments, they cast them off like outgrown playthings and never develop a taste for show and finery. The Utopians have also found a unique method for storing gold, which they use for hiring mercenaries to defend their island. To show their disdain for riches, they turn the gold into chamberpots. When they need money, they simply melt down these useful objects. Sometimes, as a particular mark of disgrace, they bind a criminal in chains of solid gold.

More, who was speaker of the House of Commons and later lord chancellor of England, has Raphael praise the few and simple laws of the land of Utopia and explain that in this ideal land there are no lawyers to confuse and distort the law. Each man pleads his own case. The criminal law is extraordinarily mild and there is no death penalty for theft. The humane customs of Utopia forbid hunting and all needless suffering is opposed. People with painful incurable illnesses are advised to commit suicide or permit euthanasia.

Sixteenth-century England was a religious battlefield, but Utopia is a land where all faiths are tolerated. The form of marriage is conventional, but a betrothed man and woman must view each other nude before making a final decision to wed. No intelligent person would buy a horse before removing saddles and blankets and assuring himself that he had seen everything and liked what he saw, More explains.

The book was written in 1516 in Latin, the language in which More could communicate with other intellectuals across national boundaries. It was translated into English in 1551 and created considerable interest immediately. Sixteen years earlier its author had been beheaded because of his opposition to King Henry VIII's marriage to Anne Boleyn.

The emphasis throughout the book, as in Plato's, is on sharing as a means to a satisfying life. Both authors agree that the happiness of men is guaranteed in a well-ordered society which provides for all their needs.

This is also the viewpoint of Edward Bellamy, an American, who in 1888 wrote his description of a perfect society in a book called *Looking Backward*. Like More's *Utopia*, *Looking Backward* promotes, as a basis for the perfect state, total social equality. Utopia becomes the United States in the year 2000 as viewed from the city of Boston. The hero of the book, Julian West, is a nineteenth-century gentleman who, one night in 1887, has himself put to sleep by a hypnotist because of his chronic insomnia. Mr. West has just returned from an evening spent with his charming financée. Fortunately, his bedroom is in a thick-walled soundproofed basement. During the night his house burns to the ground. West awakens, still snug in his basement room, to find that his deep trance has lasted rather longer than he expected. Although he is not a day older, he has slept 113 years, 3 months and 11 days. (Rip Van Winkle, another famous sleeper, only managed to snooze for two decades and awakened an old man.) Dr. Leete and his family, who live in the house which stands where West's once did, have excavated in preparation for some construction, and have hit upon the sealed basement room.

West finds that Boston has changed entirely, and he seems a bit more surprised by this fact than he might be, considering the number of years that have passed during his nap. The entire country now functions communally, with each person given an exactly equal share of each year's national product. Capitalism has been abolished and the nation owns all the means of production and distribution. Although Bellamy hated war—and abolished it in his utopian world—he calls the new national labor force the "Industrial Army." This army conscripts all men and women to work for the nation between the ages of twenty-one and forty-five. (Compulsory education lasts until age twenty-one, and compulsory retirement begins at forty-five.)

There are no employers other than the state and there are no wages. Instead of money, each person receives a credit card which is exactly equal in value to those of all other citizens, and "purchases" are made by selecting items at national storehouses. Clerks at these storehouses punch out on the consumer's card the value of his selections. Since all have the same allotment, no one tries to impress anyone else with his wealth. People may choose to apportion their income differently, however, and some prefer a larger, more imposing house than others have and are willing to spend less on other things. All work is considered equally valuable and dignified and no man thinks himself the superior of any other.

By the way, there are no taxes, there are no strikes, and there is virtually no crime, since there is no basis for desiring financial gain. The few people who commit violent acts of any sort are sent to special hospitals where their antisocial behavior is treated and cured. Women are free to work because all cooking and laundry is done in central kitchens and housework has been abolished. All look forward to their early retirement age as a time for study, for travel, for hobbies and pleasures. When they go abroad they may have their credit cards punched in a number of countries which have now followed the United States' lead and become industrial states.

Bellamy's imagination produced some fine mechanical inventions for his new world. One of these is a canopy contraption that covers all the sidewalks when it rains, so that there is no weather in which people can't go out in comfort. He also invented the clock radio. Orchestras play in distant auditoriums all day and night and you may pick them up by a connection to your telephone. An attachment is available for your clock and you can be awakened by music!

Bellamy, like all utopian writers, was strongly influenced by social and economic conditions in his own society. At the end of the nineteenth century, poverty and unemployment were the factors behind widespread industrial disturbances. Julian West is much upset by strikes which hold up his marriage and the construction of his new house. His first question on awakening in the year 2000 is: "What solution have you found for the labor problem?" Leete replies that the problem was automatically solved when the government took over the means of production and ended all possibility of unemployment or poverty. Bellamy is confident that material well-being will permit all men to live dignified and happy lives. With many other utopian writers, he believes that man is good and society evil. If society were to become good—eureka!—Utopia!!

Julian West's story ends as a tidy Victorian novel should. He woos and wins Dr. Leete's blushingly beautiful daughter Edith who turns out to be the great-great-granddaughter of his financée of 1887, also named Edith. The hero is given an appropriate position in the Industrial

Army as a professor of history. *Looking Backward* sold half a million copies within a few years of its publication and has been translated into virtually every language.

Many other utopias have been dreamed up and written down. Even in Plato's day, the playwright Aristophanes parodied utopian chatter. In the Renaissance Sir Philip Sidney contributed *Arcadia*, and Francis Bacon *New Atlantis*. Gilbert and Sullivan parodied prevalent nineteenth-century ideas in *Utopia, Ltd.*

This century has brought a number of satiric utopias or "distopias," in which seemingly admirable goals are followed to horrifyingly undesirable conclusions. In H. G. Wells's *Time Machine*, the traveler through time arrives in the year 802701 to find that man, in his search for security and freedom from toil, has evolved into two distinct creatures. The Elois are beautiful, frail-bodied, simple-minded men and women who spend their days playing, swimming, making love, adorning themselves with flowers, and dining on luscious fruits. The Morlocks, who supply all their material needs, are a grotesque and hideous race of beings who live surrounded by machines in underground caverns and who—very literally—feed on their masters, who have become enfeebled by centuries of security and ease.

Aldous Huxley, in *Brave New World*, saw modern technological progress leading to a race made up of those who controlled and those who *were* controlled. He saw people becoming robots, produced in bottles, taught to fill their role in society and kept calm and peaceful by means of drugs. George Orwell in *1984* also wrote of a strictly classed society manipulated by powerful leaders who kept their subjects brainwashed with lies. Book-burning protects people from the dangers of thinking in Ray Bradbury's *Fahrenheit 451*, where life is supposed to be sheer fun. William Golding, in *Lord of the Flies*, takes an opposite view of mankind and society to that treasured by Bellamy and most utopian writers. He puts his schoolboys on a fertile island, turns them loose, and lets the reader watch as they destroy each other because of their innate brutality. Man is corrupt, is his message—not society.

A much-discussed and controversial current utopia is presented in B. F. Skinner's *Walden II*. Skinner, a professor of psychology at Harvard, has written about a community of a thousand people in a rural area of an unnamed state. The community and its ways are described to a group of visitors, one of whom obviously represents the author. The good life, as lived in Walden II, is the result of psychological conditioning, which causes members to *want* to behave in ways that are best for themselves and for the community. Conditioning is accomplished by "positive reinforcement," which is simply a system of rewards. Wrong behavior is never punished, but right behavior is reinforced. To many critics, Skinner's theories seem to make men into machines or, almost worse, into slaves. Man, says Skinner, is shaped and controlled by outside influence, whether he likes it or not. Why not harness these techniques to teach desirable behavior?

Since infants have no inborn patterns of response, the correct rearing and education of children is central in Walden II. Infants are placed in glass boxes without clothing or blankets. Temperature and moisture are perfectly controlled. The infants remain clean and germ-free, and —since they never know discomfort—they never cry. Later, the child is carefully taught to tolerate frustration.

A lollipop, coated with powdered sugar which will show any mark, is hung around his neck. He is told that he can eat it later in the day if he does not touch it before then. Other conditioning experiments keep hungry children standing near fragrant bowls of soup for five minutes before eating, so that they'll learn self-control. All character training is completed by the age of six. The children are reared together and all adults regard all children in the community as their own.

Walden II is completely self-sufficient and everything is produced and owned communally. Everyone works on a system of "labor credits" in which less desirable jobs earn more credits than others. The number of credits required in a week permits most people to work about four hours a day, and there is plenty of leisure for the enjoyment of cultural events and the development of talents and hobbies. Marriage and childbearing begin at about age sixteen. The community is governed by planners and managers who inform themselves on issues and candidates and tell the members of the commune how to vote in local elections! A commune now in existence in Virginia is trying to make the world of Walden II an actuality.

Perhaps everyone has some fragmentary concept of what it would be like to live in a perfect world. To most it is simply a daydream; to others the vision is a challenge to action. The literature of Utopia is a vast chronicle of cherished ideals; the history of utopian communities is strangely poignant, sometimes brilliant, often zany. Perfection is an elusive goal but the search is always a reaction to the quality of life in the outside world. In America it started right at the beginning.

# 3 THE GIFT TO BE SIMPLE: THE SHAKERS AND OTHER EARLY COMMUNITARIANS

IN 1663 A GROUP of Dutch Mennonites under the leadership of one Pieter Corneliszoon Plockhoy established a settlement on a prime piece of waterfront property in the colony of New Netherlands. The exact area is now the town of Lewes, Delaware. It's tricky guesswork to speculate as to whether the community would have succeeded. A year later New Netherlands was conquered by the British, who plundered "the Quaking Society of Plockhoy to a very naile."

For the next century and a half, communal experimentation in this country was completely sectarian (religious). The great clashes in Europe during the Reformation and Counter-Reformation between the Catholics, Lutherans, and Calvinists resulted in a tangle of small dissident sects with strongly held beliefs which conflicted with the teachings of the established churches. America came to symbolize the freedom to pursue these cherished beliefs in peace. Theoretically, of course, this was so. In practice there was hardly a single instance of a religious sect which was not met with hostility by its new neighbors. The great majority of these emigrés were from Germany—most of them from the southern part of the country. Although a number of sects ultimately lived communally, this was not always the original intent. When faced with the rigors of frontier survival and the added threat posed by hostile colonists, they bound themselves together for preservation of life, of their religion, their language, and the customs of their homeland.

The Dutch Mennonites are generally considered to have been the first communitarians in America, but even earlier a missionary named John Eliot had attempted to convert the Indians to both Christianity and communal living. He taught himself to speak Algonquin and translated religious works into that language for the further edification of his chosen flock. Eliot believed that the Indians were descendants of one of the lost tribes of Israel—a belief later shared by the Mormons—and he sought to lead them into settlements which would be ordered by biblical rules for living. Records on the subject are limited, but it appears that a book Eliot wrote describing his plan so displeased the English king that it was banned, burned—and the experiment ended.

Another attempt to teach the Indians new ways was made almost a century later when Christian Priber from

Saxony went to live with the Cherokees in the southern part of the Appalachians. He learned their language and spoke to them of his thrilling plans for a community to be named Paradise. Paradise would be patterned after the utopian visions of Plato and More. What the Cherokees thought of Plato and More or of this first blueprint for a truly secular commune in America is not known. Priber was accused by the British of aiding the French and was tossed into jail where he promptly died.

One of the earliest sectarian groups, the Moravians—also known as the Renewed Church of the United Brethren—fled persecution in Bohemia and Moravia and founded a colony in Pennsylvania, the state most favored for residence because of its reputation for religious tolerance. They called their system the "General Economy." Time and labor were fed into the General Economy, and food, clothing, and shelter came forth. The impoverished Moravians arrived in 1722 and by 1754 they had four thriving colonies—three in Pennsylvania and one in North Carolina.

Some of the early communes had strange and memorable names. The most startling was the Society of the Woman in the Wilderness, so named because of the fact that in the Book of Revelation the church is described as a woman. The devout members of this settlement in Germantown, Pennsylvania, expected the arrival of the reincarnated Jesus in 1694 and they watched for signs of his coming at night with telescopes placed on the roof of the church. They lived at a high pitch of millennial fever—of expectation that the description in Revelation was about to come true and Christ would reappear to reign on earth for a thousand years. It was believed that during this millennial (thousand-year) period, the imperfections of human existence would be erased and a state of holiness and joy would prevail. The leader of the Woman in the Wilderness, Johannes Kelpius, apparently left the keeping of the watch to others. He was a hermit at heart, and when he found a natural cave nearby he moved in. He brought his books and his laboratory paraphernalia and worked at chemical experiments and started a list of Indian words in the hope of converting the nearby tribes.

Another of the early German settlements, that of the Ephratans, became the longest-lived community in American history, although it did not maintain a fully communal economic system after the eighteenth century. Established in 1732, its last few members merged into a Seventh-Day Baptist group in 1937. The Ephratans had two orders of citizens: married peasants and a separate class of celibate "Brethren" and "Spiritual Virgins." They interpreted the biblical description of Solomon's temple, which was built without hammers, axes, any iron tools, or nails, as a prohibition against the use of metal. All their tools and utensils were ingeniously fashioned of stone and wood, and they even managed to contrive a wooden implement with which to press their clothing. They also noted the biblical injunction "Narrow is the way which leadeth unto life," and followed it literally. They constructed all entrances and doorways a cramped five feet in height and twenty inches in width.

Suffering discomfort of all sorts was considered desirable and virtuous to the people of Ephrata, and stone pillows were the rule as well as coarse woollen garments, intended to chafe the skin. The holy Ephratans rose every few hours during the night for an hour of prayer, ate virtually nothing but thin gruel, and harnessed themselves to heavy wagons weighted with enormous loads. Visitors were struck by their emaciated appearance. Their first leader, the unpredictable son of an alcoholic baker, was frequently accused of committing immoral acts with the Spiritual Virgins, and yet the community survived scandals and persecutions and attracted a number of scholars. One of their members was commissioned by Congress to translate the Declaration of Independence into seven languages. Others wrote and published a number of interesting religious books and hymnals.

The first American-born communitarian was a self-styled prophet and fanatic named Shadrach Ireland, who left his wife and six children and retired to a hiding place in Harvard, Massachusetts, with a young girlfriend named Abigail Loungee whom he referred to as his "soulmate." No one really believed that their relationship was all that soulful, but he was revered as a holy man because he boasted of possessing certain very useful gifts. He could cure the sick by laying on of hands, and he also received direct revelations from the heavens. His followers, who referred to him as "The Man," built a large square communal dwelling and turned over all their possessions to their leader. The most fascinating claim Shadrach Ireland made was that he had been given an immortal body, as well as an immortal soul, and would rise after death looking just exactly as he did alive. He warned his people that if he appeared to die he was not to be buried, because he would surely come back to life on the third day. If nothing happened on the third day, he further warned, they should

expect him to awaken on the ninth. One night he did indeed give every appearance of having died. His body was
kept around for quite a while just in case, but it began to
look pretty awful. Eventually it was properly planted in a
corn field. His followers were later converted by the Shakers and their famous "Square House" in Harvard became
the central building in the Shaker village on that site.

The history of the Shakers began in eighteenth-century
England, influenced by religious developments in France.
Under the reign of Louis XIV there was considerable religious persecution of Protestants. A sect of French mystics
arose who called themselves the Camisards. Their noisy ecstatic services took the form we associate with religious
revivals. In worship, the Camisards went into seizures of
writhing. They contorted their bodies, trembled, twitched,
called out in strange tongues, and fell into trances.

In 1705 a group of these French Camisards emigrated to
England. Two English Quakers, James and Jane Wardley,
who lived near Manchester, had left the Society of Friends
after being influenced by the Camisards. The Wardleys
and their small group of believers were dubbed "Shaking
Quakers" or "Shakers" by their scornful neighbors, who
saw in their noisy and athletic form of worship the influence of the devil and not that of the Christian God. What
really outraged nonbelievers was the Shakers' prediction
that Jesus would reappear in the form of a woman. They
not only predicted her coming, but they eagerly awaited
her arrival because they expected her *soon*. God, they said,
had a two-sided nature—male and female. Jesus had been
the male manifestation, and the female member would
usher in the millennium.

During this period a pious young girl grew up in the

brutal working-class slums of Manchester on a street named—horribly—Toad Lane. She had no schooling whatsoever, and at about the age of fourteen went to work as a velvet cutter and hatter's helper in the textile mills. Perhaps it was because of tales she heard or sights she witnessed, or perhaps she had some alarming experiences— no one knows—but from an early age she had a total aversion to the sexual act. She pleaded with her mother to permit her to remain unmarried and spent all her free time worshipping with the members of the Wardleys' society. To her great misery, her sympathetic mother died, and Ann's father forced her into marriage with a man who, like himself, was a blacksmith. The marriage license, signed with an "x" by both parties, still exists. Within as many years, Ann was delivered of four children in a series of difficult labors, and each of the children died either at birth or in infancy. To the young woman, this was evidence of God's judgment against sexual union.

Night after night Ann prayed to God to deliver her from sin. Her anguished groans were heard the length of Toad Lane. She trembled in her penitence and her body oozed blood instead of sweat, or so it is written. She ate almost nothing and became alarmingly thin. During the years of this religious ordeal she attended meetings with the Wardleys and suffered stonings by mobs and every variety of physical abuse. She and the Wardleys were accused of blasphemy and heresy and on one occasion the magistrate threatened to have a hole bored through her tongue with a hot iron, which was the way they dealt with heretics thereabouts. It is said that she was saved from this dreadful fate by going into an inspired trance in which she spoke in seventy-two different languages. The jurors were so impressed that they tossed her in jail and tried to starve her to death instead.

Ann's period in jail was to lead to her elevation as a holy person and a martyr. Her jailers fed her nothing, but a young disciple dripped milk and wine through a pipestem which he injected through a crack in the wall at night. While in prison she experienced a great vision. When she was released she announced to her Shaker friends, "I spoke with Christ!" This time the Wardleys were impressed. Christ had instructed her, it seems, to preach virginity and purity to her people. He had given her a vision of Adam and Eve in the Garden of Eden and had shown her their act of physical love and declared that this was the cause of man's fall. He had also informed her that she was the new incarnation of Christ, the female member of the Godhead.

After this she was known as Ann the Word, Ann Christ, and Mother Ann. The society of Shakers took the official name of The United Society of Believers in Christ's Second Appearing and adopted the doctrine that the second appearing had now occurred—in the person of humble Ann Lee of Toad Lane.

After this the persecutions increased. Ann was dragged downstairs and through the streets. She and her people were beaten and imprisoned with grim regularity, until it appeared that Ann Christ might not survive to spread the joyous word that the earth was now heaven and mankind was saved.

At the age of thirty-eight she was given a second major vision in which she was told to take her people to America and establish in this new land the True Church. On the ship crossing the Atlantic, the captain was so outraged by the Shakers' stamping and whirling and shouting that he threatened to throw them into the sea, but when a wave loosened a board and the ship began to fill with water, Ann assured him that all would be well. Soon another wave, seemingly by a miracle, pushed the board exactly into place.

Upon arrival in America Ann took work as a housemaid, her followers found similar jobs, and her rejected husband found a position as a smith. He made no secret of his fury at his wife's sexual attitudes and he left her soon afterward for a "lewd woman." No one quite understood why he had tagged along to begin with. An inexpensive tract of land was found near Albany, New York, and soon a two-story cabin was erected, one floor for the "sisters" and one for the "brethren."

From this fragile and unlikely beginning, the great flowering of Shaker life unfolded. Americanization was rapid. Ann and her followers left their settlement, which was surrounded by Indians, mainly Iroquois, and went on a two-year trip around New England, urging people to make confession of sins, give up sex, and come to live with them as loving brothers and sisters. The Shakers were dragged by the hair, beaten with clubs, and terrorized by ruffians along their route. It was the time of the Revolutionary War and these British emigrés were accused of treason as well as of witchcraft. Since they preached pacifism they were charged with being British spies, sent to undermine the American fighting spirit. The Shakers, who cared nothing for politics and world affairs, continued spreading the word, teaching little children songs about the depravity of marriage, assuring all that ecstasy was to be found in the life of self-denial rather than in the life of self-indulgence. In Harvard, Mother Ann tried to convert the ghost of Shadrach Ireland, believing that even the dead could be saved, but she found him an impossibly stubborn spirit. Ann also spoke of everyday matters. She remained a simple woman who preached the value of honest labor and of neatness and of kindness. She urged people to bring up children with gentleness in a period when this was not very common.

At about the time the first Shaker communes were being established, another female prophet was making trips about the countryside seeking converts. Jemima Wilkinson, a beautiful woman from Rhode Island, was twenty years old in 1780 when she became very ill and then seemed to stop breathing. All through the next forty-eight hours, during which time she had the good fortune to be left in her bed, she was visited with visions of angels who informed her that she was about to be resurrected in the body of the Holy One and to be given Jesus' duty of judging men until his second coming. When she awakened and rose from her bed she announced that she was now to be known as the Publick Universal Friend—and many people listened. There was a doctor in the case, who was of the opinion that she had merely suffered a feverish delirium, but Jemima forever afterward insisted her soul had gone to heaven—and returned.

She led her followers to the Genesee Valley of New York and set up a community named Jerusalem. Her carriage was painted with the words, "The Universal Friend." She wore an odd costume, topped by a broad-brimmed hat, that reminded people of a riding habit. She was described as tall, black-eyed, and fine-featured, and several hundred followers handed over their worldly goods to her and proclaimed her Christ. Although it was believed that she, like many other prophets, would live forever, she died in 1820, and her clan dispersed soon afterwards. The Shakers denounced her as a charlatan—a less than mediocre imitation of Mother Ann.

Ann Lee died only eight years after her arrival in America, but, unlike the "Jemimakins" and countless other short-lived sects, the Shakers never seemed to lack capable leaders. No sect became totally Americanized, flourished, grew, and prospered like the Shakers. Within ten years of the arrival of the English Shakers in 1776, leadership had passed entirely and permanently into American hands. By the turn of the century there were ten Shaker communes in New York and New England, each divided into "families" of about fifty men and women. In 1805 a group went forth to the wild west of Kentucky, Ohio, and Indiana, picking up large numbers of Revivalist converts. Five more villages were founded. Not long afterward a commune was established in Ohio in the area which is now the Shaker Heights suburb of Cleveland. By 1827 there were five thousand Shakers living in seventeen large and prosperous Shaker villages in eight states. The peak of six thousand members was reached in the 1840s—the golden age of the communal movement.

Where did the Shakers fit into the early history of religious communalism? Unlike the members of the foreign-language sects, they immediately set about seeking American converts. Furthermore, they succeeded, and because of this success, they became the first group to be regarded as a genuine menace. Although Mennonites and Moravians and Ephratans suffered considerable harassment, the Shakers underwent the most severe persecutions. The dangers they realistically feared and the cruel indignities repeatedly inflicted upon them in their first years in America were the forces that quickly led to their adoption of a fully communitarian way of life.

It is not at all easy to comprehend why the Shakers were able to attract so many converts. Since their faith absolutely prohibited sexual union, their survival and growth depended entirely on attracting new members, and their efforts to do so were continuous. Ever charitable, the Shakers adopted large groups of orphans, but only an estimated 10 percent of these stayed with the community as adults. The rest, upon reaching their teens or early adulthood, began to resent their narrow lives and conspicuous clothes, their routine days and the restrictions of the faith. Furthermore, the Shaker villages offered no entertainment or recreation whatsoever. The world beckoned alluringly and they ventured out, some in terror and some with a sense of joyous release. It was the adult converts who came and kept coming right through the years until the general national decrease in communal living after the Civil War.

Certainly the basic religious beliefs of the Shakers must have been as difficult for some converts of the eighteenth and nineteenth century to accept as they would be for us today. There were two major points of doctrine. First: their founder, Ann Lee, a mill worker from Manchester, England, was the second incarnation of God, the first having been Jesus of Nazareth. What this meant to those awaiting the millennium, of course, was that the millennium had actually arrived, that the promised one thousand years of heaven on earth had begun—and that everyone was saved. Second: brotherly and sisterly love are in every way superior to married love; sex is the source of most of the evil in the world. In the early years, it was also essential to accept the notion that religious belief is best expressed by a form of worship involving shaking, twitching, screaming, trancing, barking, and whirling about in circles.

If much of what the Shakers believed seems bizarre to us today, and if their lives appear to have been bare and spare and boring, the fact still remains that they attracted newcomers from virtually every religious group and secular movement in existence during their long history. Those who didn't join came to observe. All the important people associated with communal experiments in the nineteenth century—Robert Owen, George Ripley, Bronson Alcott, John Humphrey Noyes—visited the Shakers, and most left imbued with sincere admiration. President James Monroe visited a Shaker village in New Hampshire in 1817 and later he and Andrew Jackson traveled to another in Kentucky. Alexis de Tocqueville, the author of *Democracy in America*, included an account of the Shakers in his monumental classic. The great number of European visitors in the nineteenth century was a reflection of socialist concerns which led to far-reaching political upheaval in Germany and France in 1848. Late in the century, Leo Tolstoy, another visionary, carried on a lengthy correspondence concerning the sect with a Shaker leader.

Few intellectuals of the era ridiculed the Shakers. Charles Dickens was an exception. On his triumphal

American tour, he made a point of visiting a Shaker village just five days before he embarked to return to England. His record can be found in his *American Notes*. He was not charmed by what he saw. "We walked into a grim room where several grim hats were hanging on grim pegs, and the time was grimly told by a grim clock, which uttered every tick with a kind of struggle as if it broke the grim silence reluctantly and under protest. Ranged against the wall were six or eight stiff highbacked chairs, and they partook so strongly of the general grimness, that one would much rather have sat on the floor then incurred the slightest obligation to any of them." Presently a man appeared, "a grim old Shaker, with eyes as hard and dull and cold as the great round metal buttons of his waistcoat; a sort of calm goblin." When Dickens went to buy some Shaker handicrafts he was assisted by "something alive in a russet case, which the elder said was a woman; and which I supposed *was* a woman, though I should not have suspected it." Although he was not able to witness a religious service, he imagined it as "unspeakably absurd" and "infinitely grotesque." He left with a "hearty dislike of the old Shakers and a hearty pity for the young ones."

What the Shakers offered, in the crisis-ridden society of the Industrial Revolution, was a way of life that was peaceful, orderly, secure, and humane. In a Shaker village everything was immaculately neat and clean, meals were ample and regular, everyone was kind to everyone else, and all people were respected. It is statistically proven that they lived healthier and longer lives than people in the outside world. Elders and eldresses of eighty were common, and many lived even longer, in a period when this was extremely rare. Although Shakers worked regularly they never worked to excess, and their many agricultural and craft projects permitted great opportunity for variety of endeavor. To be equipped to alternate jobs, all Shakers learned several trades or crafts as well as agriculture.

There were always many more women than men in the Shaker villages and their status was that of total equality. In an age when women had few rights, when they were frequently married off by parental arrangement to men they disliked, when so many young women died in childbirth—the sexless, marriageless, and protected life offered by the Shakers did not seem such a dire alternative to the struggle in the outside world. Among both the male and female converts were Negroes who joined the Shakers both before and after emancipation, and who were welcomed as total equals. No other early communes could compete in this area, nor did they try.

Refugees from other sects joined but converts also came from strictly nonreligious communes. Many followers of Robert Owen, whose ideology was definitely antireligious, joined the Shakers after the collapse of New Harmony and its several offshoot communes. Members of Adventist William Miller's group, who had given away all their worldly goods in expectation of the Lord's coming in 1843, turned in disillusion, poverty, and despair to the Shakers.

It must also be recognized that to many nineteenth-century men and women, communitarian living was a lifetime commitment which sent people wandering from one experiment to another. This floating group formed a major source of Shaker membership. Communal arrangements were constantly folding and members, set adrift, would look for another association. The substantial and enduring Shaker villages were an obvious refuge, especially since social and economic security were increasingly emphasized over religious belief as the years went on.

Life in the villages did not change greatly over the decades. Everyone arose at 4:30 A.M. in the summer and an hour later in winter. They went to bed at 9:00 after a bit of chatter and prayers. To the Shakers every day was the Sabbath and worship was a way of life, but the old methods in which each worshipper went into his own frenzy changed, and the men and women were taught ritual religious dances which were performed in unison. Members of the outside world came to watch these dances and to listen to the new Shaker hymns. Singing was also rehearsed and the ban on musical instruments was eventually lifted.

Shaker men and women never touched, and all Shaker dormitories had two staircases, one for the males and one for the females, so that they need not pass on the stairs and perhaps brush one another by accident. (Staircases, of course, were very narrow in earlier times.) All doors were double, providing one entry for either sex. Clothing was extremely simple and modest. Women wore, at all times, a kerchief over the shoulders and chest which was designed to conceal the shape of the breasts. They wore snug caps both indoors and out to hide what might be attractive hair. Outdoors they also wore deep sunbonnets. Blue and white checkered aprons covered long simple skirts in pale colors. Sometimes white with a delicate blue stripe was worn in summer. The brethren wore blue coats with capes, breeches, and brass-buckled shoes on Sunday, but on other days their costumes were more drab. Although styles changed slightly over the years, at any given time exact uniformity in style and color was the rule. It was considered important to the maintenance of social and economic equality.

Shaker farm produce was reputed to be of the highest quality. The Shakers were famous for seeing that the top, middle, and bottom layers in boxes of fruit and vegetables were exactly the same. It is recorded that they were even perfectly honest in horse trading!

The sisters and the brethren worked in separate shops turning out a great number of products. The simple ladderback chairs were perfectly fashioned in every detail. Shakers never aimed for beauty in their designs—only utility—and yet their chairs are much more beautiful to our twentieth-century eyes than many of the overly ornate furnishings made for wealthy homes of the period. Today they are collectors' items.

Bottled and boxed herbal medicines were the Shakers' most profitable venture until 1930 when they stopped the manufacture of drugs under new laws covering patent medicines. At one time they sold two hundred extracts of herbs, barks, roots, and berries. They made and sold fine woollen cloaks, blankets, carpets, straw bonnets, and wool hats. For some years they were the largest producers of flowers and vegetable seeds in the country. They made distinctive brooms and brushes, saddles and harnesses and shoes, spinning wheels, wagons, clocks, wooden dippers, tubs, baskets and pipes and cushions and fans and gloves. They were ingenious at making and adopting labor-saving devices and are credited with the invention of the circular saw, the common clothespin, a rotary harrow, a threshing machine, an apple-coring gadget, a pea-sheller, and many other mechanical devices.

The changes in the outside world had very little influence on Shaker life, although the Shakers instituted evening sessions in which elders and eldresses read aloud preselected portions of the daily newspaper. Nothing concerning sex or war or any other offensive subject was included. The troubles of others often touched them deeply. When they read about the Irish famine they sent generous financial aid. When they brought to White House attention the fact that Shaker converts who were Revolutionary War veterans had routinely refused to accept their pensions, Lincoln ordered the Shakers who had been imprisoned for refusing to serve in the Civil War released.

As the end of the century approached, it became more and more difficult to keep the children down on the farm. Schooling was meager, social contacts with the world's people were nil. Increasing numbers of young people who wanted to marry ran off together. Many young men left to join the military forces in the Civil War. Financial problems arose as the products of Shaker artisan tradition failed to compete in a changing industrialized society. Fires, property damage in the Kentucky village during the war, and financial mismanagement by senile elders resulted in devastating losses. After the Civil War the number of people leaving the villages increased rapidly and no new converts arrived. An attempt in 1894 to start a village in Narcosee, Florida, failed to attract a single member. When the production of medicinal herbs stopped in the 1930s, Shaker women began making pathetic little pincushions and souvenirs which they peddled in New England summer resorts. The Shaker villages were emptying out and families were moved from one to another as they closed down.

The last Shaker chair was carved and joined in 1947. Imitations lack the qualities of workmanship and exquisite simplicity of design that make Shaker furniture loved by connoisseurs. Examples can be seen in museums—the Smithsonian Institution in Washington, D.C., the Boston Museum of Fine Arts, the Winterthur Museum in Delaware, the Cincinnati Art Museum, the Philadelphia Museum of Art, and many others. There are also exhibits in the Shaker Historical Society Museum in the Shaker Heights area of Cleveland and at the Shaker Museum in Old Chatham, New York.

Two Shaker communities have been restored, to the delight of thousands of visitors. The village in Hancock, Massachusetts, has seventeen original buildings and the village in Pleasant Hills, Kentucky, has twenty-two. Fourteen Shaker sisters are still living, although the last Shaker brother died in 1961. The sisters live in two communities —one in Canterbury, New Hampshire, and one in Sabbathday Lake, Maine, both of which were founded in 1782. As they walk in and out of their dining and sitting rooms through the old double doors, the sisters still use the one on the left. Male visitors and caretakers use the door to the right. The elderly ladies repeat the old sayings and sing the old songs with joy because, as one of them has written, "Regardless of our numbers or our age, we have what the world is seeking and it will yet come into its own."

# 4

## ON THE BANKS OF THE WABASH: GEORGE RAPP AND HIS FOLLOWERS

THE MOST REMARKABLE SIGHT in the rugged wilds of the new state of Indiana in the decade following the War of 1812 was a town on the banks of the broad River Wabash which was sweetly named Harmonie.

Eight hundred people lived in this settlement, and to the eyes of the astounded travelers who passed that way, it looked precisely like a quaint and immaculate German village magically set down in a sparsely populated wilderness. Sturdy stone buildings, two-story brick and timber residences, and a vast church in the shape of a cross bordered the gracious tree-lined square. A brass band oompah-pahed merrily on a hillside while men in the fields scythed as much as one hundred acres of wheat in a day. Pots of fresh flowers from the town's gardens and greenhouses sat on each machine in the small trim factories and on the looms in the mills.

The church was indeed a most remarkable structure. It measured 120 feet in each direction and had twenty-eight massive Doric columns of sassafras, cherry, and walnut supporting a fine dome. Its tower housed a resonant brass bell from England and was topped with a balcony from which the band blared marches and hymns during the warm evenings. The plans for this church had been dictated directly from heaven to the community's absolute ruler, George Rapp, who received them in great detail in a dream. It was built to the specifications he set down, and when it was finished, he himself carved and gilded a large rose—the symbol of the millennium—which was placed over the doorway.

Rapp—who was known to all as Father Rapp— slept well in his grand stone residence, which boasted two lightning rods and basement tunnels offering access by underground routes to the church and the town's second most impressive building, a granary. The granary was built with a tile roof and walls of stone two feet thick as effective protection against weevils. It also served as storage house for rifles and ammunition, having been designed for alternative use as a fort in the event of invasion from the hostile outside world.

Although the granary was never actually required for defense, the hostility of the outside world toward the Rappites was real enough. It was firmly based on envy, on intolerance, on moral disapproval. Compared with the lives of privation endured by the rowdy squatters and trappers who were their neighbors, the Rappites dwelt snugly in comfort and security in their picture-book village. Furthermore, although they lived communally and no man or woman among them had any private income or property, they were, as a group, enormously wealthy. Their jointly owned houses, shops, land, livestock, mills, distilleries, and their manufactured products and crops were valued at over a million dollars, while the average total worth per capita in Indiana was $150. They were heartily fed, simply but warmly clothed, and housed in tightly constructed residences. Their shops held the monopoly on trade throughout the region and their wealth brought them considerable influence in high places. When the territory of Indiana became a state in 1816, an annual period of militia duty was required of all men aged eighteen to fifty. The fine for absence was set at seventy-five cents a day. The Rappites, who refused to serve, managed to have the fine reduced for their men, through the intercession of their leader's adopted son, Frederick, who had served on the committee which framed the first state constitution. This did not increase their popularity in the new American democracy.

Although the prosperity of the community excited envy, it also aroused reluctant admiration. Neighbors and visitors puzzled and watched and studied in hopes of finding a clue which would turn their own poverty into prosperity. Two major features of life in Harmonie, however, inspired simple unadulterated scorn in the outside world: the Rappites' refusal to assimilate and their rule of celibacy. It was frequently announced that no "good American" would dream of joining the ranks of these foreigners. Indeed, there is little evidence that any sought admission, and strong indication that had they done so, they would not have been welcomed. Although the Rappites had fled religious persecution in Germany and conscription in Napoleon's army, they had by no means left their European tastes behind. They retained their simple German peasant garb and their native language. George Rapp himself never mastered English, although he lived in this country for forty years. Trade with the outside world made it necessary for some members of the community to learn the new language, but reading, writing, and conversation in Harmonie were always in German. As a religious group they never proselytized and, although they ran an inn which accommodated travelers, requests from outsiders to attend church services and queries about their ways and beliefs were sternly rebuffed. Positive attempts to isolate themselves from their fellow Indianians were made when they bought up large tracts of land surrounding their fields.

Celibacy was a major feature of their differentness. In the village of Harmonie, husbands and wives lived together and young men and women worked alongside each other in the fields, but year after year virtually no children were born because Father Rapp had decreed that sexual relations were an abomination to the Lord, and whatever Father Rapp ordered or prohibited became the law in Harmonie. Some historians contend that there was not a single breach of this rule in the entire hundred-year history of the Rappites. Others report a few backsliders. In a period of twenty years a dozen children are said to have been born unhappy living witnesses to their parents' carnal natures and their unwillingness to obey Father Rapp. Tales of this community of sexual abstainers spread back to Eu-

rope, and Lord Byron posed his mystification in the fif-
teenth canto of *Don Juan:*

> When Rapp the Harmonist embargo'd marriage
> In his harmonious settlement—(which flourishes
> Strangely enough as yet without miscarriage,
> Because it breeds no more mouths than it nourishes,
> Without those sad expenses which disparage
> What Nature naturally most encourages)—
> Why call'd he "Harmony" a state sans wedlock?
> Now here I have got the preacher at a dead lock.

The Harmonists' neighbors expressed their view less ele-
gantly. They were repelled by the notion of celibacy
among married men and women and painted obscene in-
scriptions on the walls of Rappites' homes. They expressed
horror at what they considered the community's ignorance, superstition, and slavish obedience to Rapp. Rapp,
who to his people was a holy man elected to leadership by
God, seemed to many outsiders a tyrant and fanatic. It is
said that one night a man dressed in a nightshirt galloped
through the village astride a white horse shouting through
the childless streets that God loved little children. It is also
said that he was well fortified against the cold with the po-
tent product of the Rappites' Golden Rule Distillery.

How did this band of industrious Germans find their
way to the American Midwest and what was the basis of
their beliefs? Their new life began in Württemberg in
1803 when a forty-eight-year-old vineyard worker and lay
preacher named George Rapp received the divine command to lead his followers to America.

Rapp was the son of a family of vine planters. He was a tall, strong peasant as a young man in Germany. His portrait, painted in America when he was quite old, shows a powerful patriarchal face framed by a heavy white beard. He called himself a Lutheran, as did most of his followers, but he preached that the established church ignored the teachings of Christ. He refused to perform military service and urged those who listened to his sermons to do likewise. Farmers who came to his house in Württemberg to hear him expound on the words of Jesus and his apostles found themselves hauled off to jail on the next day. As a Lutheran, Rapp believed that every Christian was entitled to preach, but he lived in a period of bitter religious intolerance. In 1799, he was imprisoned for driving a herd of pigs through the streets of town while God-fearing folks were at church services. Such services, he told the judge, were a mockery abhorrent to the Lord and only served the interests of the devil. Four years later, having attracted a large group of converts to his sect, he left Germany to found in America a community of believers who would be free to save their own souls by living the life God decreed, as revealed through his messenger, George Rapp.

Rapp never acknowledged any written document except the Bible. From his interpretations of various passages he deduced that the millennium would come within his lifetime and that he himself would present his people to the Lord on the occasion of his Second Coming. To prepare for this day, he believed that, like the early Christians, his people must give up all private property and live by sharing. He cited as God's word on communal living the thirty-second verse of the fourth chapter of Acts: "And the multitude of them that believed were of one heart and of one soul: neither said any of them that ought of the things which he possessed was his own; but they had all things common." A careful reading of Genesis revealed to Rapp that before the Fall Adam was celibate. Since Adam was created in God's image, Rapp's deduction was that God favored—yea, commanded—celibacy as a necessary part of the preparation for the millennium. The rule also had a sound economic basis. Without children there would be less burden on the new community both for funds and for attention. Women would be free to work in the fields with men, and loyalty to the community and its work would not be diluted by time and attention directed toward family interests. Although most of the men and women who followed Rapp to the new land were already married young adults with families—Father Rapp himself was a widower with a son and a daughter—his rule of abstinence in the new life was accepted by the great majority. Most of those who found themselves unwilling to deny the pleasures and rights of marital love and parenthood soon left the group.

The first Rappite village was established in 1804 in Pennsylvania on forty-five hundred acres of land northwest of Pittsburgh. Auspiciously, the immigrants landed on July 4, and from that year on extended rare hospitality on Independence Day to outsiders, who were invited to join in large doses of food, beer, and band music, and to hear patriotic speeches, delivered in German, which praised the freedom of the New World while reminding the community members to strive always to preserve their own ways and traditions.

Upon arrival in Pennsylvania, the immigrants immediately began to clear the land and construct log houses. Articles of association of the society were drawn up declaring that all property was to be given over to Rapp and other leaders he designated, who would use it only for the benefit of the community. His subjects agreed to obey the rules of the leader and to work for the common welfare. Rapp assumed the responsibility of providing clothing, food, and lodging, and guaranteed to care for the elderly, the sick, and the orphaned children of any members who died.

Within a year vineyards had been planted; a sawmill, a tannery, a woollen mill, and a distillery were in full operation; and Rapp regretted the fact that his land was twelve miles from the river on which his goods were to be transported for marketing. In 1806, dressed in his pantaloons and blue jacket and odd flat peasant hat, he traveled to Washington to request easy credit terms on a thirty-thousand-acre tract of undeveloped government-owned land further west.

The document he presented to President Thomas Jefferson still exists. He describes his people as "chiefly cultivators of the Vine, which last occupation they contemplate as their primary object" and states that their present tract of land in Pennsylvania is "too small, too brocken and too cold to raise Vine." Explaining that they did not have the funds to purchase the land at that time, Rapp tells Jefferson that when his people sold their property in Germany "they got scarce half the value of it"; that they had "a good deal unwealthy people" among them; that they paid cash for their present acreage, and that two thousand dollars went for cattle the first year and for the food necessary to sustain their people and livestock until their land began producing. A Senate bill granted land in the Indiana Territory on the most liberal terms imaginable—two dollars down and credit without interest for six years— but a tie vote in the House of Representatives was broken by a dissenter, who pointed out that veterans of the Revolution had a greater right to government largess than aliens, and that—furthermore—wine-drinking was really an unhealthy pastime of Europeans and not an American custom at all, so why encourage it?

It was eight years before the Rappites, despite their great talent for money-making, were able to buy the wondrously fertile land on the Wabash. They sold the Pennsylvania property, encouraged a new group of immigrants from Germany to join them in Indiana, and, having loaded their goods on barges which took them down the Ohio to the mouth of the Wabash, began at once to construct permanent dwellings of brick and stone in their land of Harmonie. Malaria was rampant and, since Rapp, on no scientific evidence, believed that Lombardy poplars repelled the disease, he lined the town with these tall trees. Despite this precaution, there were many deaths from the illness during the first years.

Harmonie was a beautifully successful project in city planning. The houses, built like those in the homeland, opened to the side rather than to the street, and were solidly constructed utilizing unique prefabricated sections put together at the mill. There were conveniently located public wells and communal ovens, and flowers and herbs grew in neatly tended rows along each street. There were forty private dwellings, four large dormitories housing sixty to eighty unmarried men or women each, and many log cabins. The church and granary were the most prominent buildings but there were many others: stores, a tavern, a tannery, a hat-making establishment, an apothecary, a hospital, a dye works, a brewery, and two distilleries. There was a sheepfold and a large piggery, a cider and wine press, a saddler's establishment, a ropery, a cotton factory, horse stables. There were greenhouses where a steady temperature was maintained all year and Father Rapp grew fig, lemon, and orange trees. There was a cocoonery where silkworms did their dainty work, and there was a silk factory. Since many of the new arrivals had children, there was even a schoolhouse which offered lessons in German for children aged six to fourteen. There was a goose meadow and a deer park, and fruits grew abundantly in the orchards. Large dogs walked treadwheels to pump water into the brewery. Houses were meticulously scrubbed in the best tradition of German housewifery and were furnished with austerely beautiful Shaker chairs and tables which the Harmonists purchased from their fellow communitarians.

There were a number of unique points of sightseeing interest in town. Rapp had a great fascination with horticulture, and not only did he grow all types of flowers and tropical fruits, but he constructed an enormous maze of hedges in which delighted wanderers could lose themselves for hours before hitting on the turns which would lead them to the fanciful little temple in its center. The labyrinth, Rapp explained, represented the difficult route to salvation. A huge sundial was another curiosity, and most exotic of all was a stone in Rapp's garden which bore the impression of two slightly larger than man-sized feet. It was said by the Harmonists that the angel Gabriel had descended—placing his left foot slightly ahead of the right—to speak to Rapp on matters of mutual concern. It is now thought that Rapp, on a trip to St. Louis— where the footprints had been observed in earlier years —brought the stone back with him. It is not known whether he related the story of the angel's visit to his credulous flock or whether the legend became popular after his death.

Life in Harmonie was certainly orderly and peaceful. The people were awakened by the sound of horns and ate breakfast. They marched singing, out to the fields, behind the band. They worked a twelve-hour day on the crops, in the mills and the orchards, the brickyard, the distillery, but their toil was interrupted by five daily meals: breakfast at six, a mid-morning brunch at nine, dinner at noon, hearty snacking at three and supper at six or seven. Each evening before sunset all sinners came to Father Rapp, who heard their confessions. He also preached at church several times weekly. After supper the band played, the childless men and women strolled in the maze and the pleasure gardens. Curfew was at nine and was signaled by the call of the night watch: "A day is past and a step made nearer our end. Our time runs away, and the joys of heaven are our reward." With this reminder everyone went to sleep.

Clothing was uniform: pantaloons, long jackets, and flat hats in a deep shade of blue for the men, petticoats and jackets and little peaked black caps which tied under the chin for the women. In the summer the women wore gray cotton dresses and both sexes wore straw hats which were manufactured in the town. A visitor commented scornfully on the "ugliness" of the Rappite women, who worked in the fields and dressed alike and pulled their hair straight up under their straw hats, making no effort whatsoever to pretty themselves or attract a man's eye.

Although the Rappite whiskey was a great success with Americans, the people of Harmonie drank only beer and wine, and even then in rationed moderation. Father Rapp dispersed both from a storeroom located in his own house. Tobacco was entirely forbidden among the members. Although their cottons and woollens and silks were alleged to be of the highest quality, these industrious celibates wore only rough durable fabrics.

Their products were sold throughout the Mississippi Valley. Early attempts to market wine and mutton in a whiskey-drinking and beef- and pork-eating land failed, but their highly desirable produce included every sort of fruit, wheat, oats, corn, hides and furs, saddles, wagons, butter and honey, cider, hogs, geese, horses, logs, whiskey, beer, and many types of cloth. The Harmonists were reluctant to sell their whiskey to their rough, tough, and unfriendly neighbors. They shipped it far away, as far as New Orleans. They had agents in Pittsburgh, St. Louis, and other large cities, and branch stores up and down the river.

After a decade of great prosperity in Indiana, the Rappites moved again, this time to a piece of land in Pennsylvania on the Ohio River. Why Rapp decided to abandon Harmonie to build a new town, which would be named Economie, is not entirely clear, but he knew his people well. Life in Harmonie had become routine and secure, and people were beginning to ask why they were forbidden to rest a bit and enjoy the fruits of their labor. Some few whispered of how nice it might be to drink some of the fine whiskey they brewed; of how delightful it would be to dress in the high-quality woollens and silks from their mills; and wasn't it time they had a shorter working day? A former member had brought a lawsuit to recover wages for labor and services rendered. The case was decided against him, since in signing the articles of association he was judged to have renounced all claim to such payment, but questions began to trouble the minds of those whose faith was wavering. Rapp knew that the necessary labor of building a new town would put an end to the sins that can breed in idleness.

In August of 1824, the Rappites loaded household goods, provisions, and tools on a steamboat. The first group to reach Economie built a steamboat to transport the rest of their people and possessions and a large stock of gold. The steamboat was named the *William Penn*, and among the last inhabitants loaded aboard were the faithful dogs who had worked the treadmill. The only item left behind was a handsome fire wagon. It simply wouldn't fit on the boat. Harmonie was sold to a man from Scotland named Robert Owen who would rename it New Harmony and establish there a second utopia of an entirely different nature.

Economie was laid out exactly like Harmonie. A new maze was constructed, and even a Chinese grotto. A museum was built and filled chock-full of Indian beads and moccasins and tomahawks and pottery and odd specimens of shells and minerals. Again, the most impressive private residence was that of Father Rapp. In his dining room hung a painting of Christ healing the sick by the most famous painter of the time, Benjamin West. It was much admired by the Duke of Saxe-Weimar, who visited Economie in 1826. The duke also reported that Rapp's table was set with delicate china and heavy silver and that a servant prepared the fine meals.

Rapp's household comprised his daughter, Rosina, his adopted son, Frederick, and a granddaughter, Gertrude, who had been born to his son John and his wife in the New World after the rule of celibacy took effect. John himself died suddenly and mysteriously just before the colony moved to Indiana. Persistent rumors held that he had been murdered by his father because of his sexual indulgence. Visitors from Europe told of having heard the story in Germany. Frederick, who was responsible for much of the business success of the community, was to die in 1836, and again it would be said that he had been assassinated by Father Rapp. Others claimed a large tree fell on him accidentally in the forest. The truth of both deaths lies buried in unmounded unmarked Rappite graves.

The Duke of Saxe-Weimar was astounded by the warmth Rapp's subjects showed their ruler. He described an evening's entertainment in which sixty or seventy Rappite girls sang in concert, with Rapp placed lovingly in the center of the group. He wrote that all Rapp's people greeted him as a father and expressed great affection and respect for their ruler-priest. The duke also described the good health of the people and the pipes connected with a steam engine which warmed the workshops and factories. At this time the colony had reached its highest census of one thousand inhabitants.

Only five years later a great tragedy occurred which almost resulted in the dissolution of the community. A man who called himself Count Maximilian de Leon, but who was, in fact, a traveling salesman from Frankfort named Bernard Mueller, arrived in Economie in full regal garb with a retinue of forty followers. He had written Rapp from Germany a year before, speaking of his great interest in the Rappite religious beliefs and communitarian life and giving himself the preposterously grand title, "The Ambassador and Anointed of God, of the Stem of Judah, of the Root of David." It is difficult to imagine how he won the confidence of clever Father Rapp, who sent him enthusiastic messages of welcome. The entire town of Economie lined the streets leading to the church as the masquerader made his appearance. True, he was a bit fatter than expected in a man of such single-minded piety, and indeed people were a bit shocked to find that there was also a "Countess Leon" and a small daughter, but no one spotted him as an imposter. He was led by Rapp himself to the pulpit, where he read to the excited populace from his "Golden Book." The golden sayings written in the book were his own, and, in concluding his remarks, he announced that his reception from Father Rapp that day was the most significant meeting since the creation.

The bogus count set up housekeeping at the inn and in short time his treachery became apparent. He chided the people on their blind obedience to Rapp. He assured them that they deserved greater personal comforts. Most important of all, he preached the end of celibacy, and enjoyment of the privileges of the marital bed. He succeeded in appealing to all Rappites who were in any way disaffected with the movement. He called for a show of loyalty and a third of the members of the society voted to make him head of the association. Rapp replied with a line from Revelation: "And the tail of the dragon drew the third part of the stars of heaven, and did cast them to earth."

Rapp was faced with his first and only major crisis. He knew that Mueller must be expelled, and he offered $105,000 to the charlatan to take those who would follow him and go far far away from the town of Economie. Almost two hundred Rappites chose to leave with the new prophet, but they didn't go far. They founded a new commune ten miles down the Ohio River and set about establishing a honeymoon haven. Within a year they had no money left and a contingent of eighty-eight "Leonists" returned to Economie in an attempt to extract more money from Rapp, who, in bitterness and anger, drove them away at once to the accompaniment of fife and drums. Soon afterward a disastrous fire totally destroyed Economie's huge woollen factory. The Leonists had threatened to do precisely this, and since there was no candle, chimney, or fire in the building, arson was almost certainly the cause.

Finding themselves without sustenance, the Leonists migrated to Louisiana, to an area which the count said had the same latitude as Jerusalem and was a likely spot for Christ to choose for the Second Coming. He died of cholera while waiting, and the colony eked out a survival for thirty-five more years before it dissolved. The "countess" retired to Hot Springs, Arkansas.

Rapp died in 1847 at the age of ninety. So unshaken was his faith that he would personally introduce his people to the Lord that, on the night of his death, he said to one who watched by the bedside, "If I did not so fully believe that the Lord has designed me to place our society before his presence in the land of Canaan, I would consider this night to be my last." His followers had also kept the faith and had never imagined their ruler would die before the Lord's coming. Many expected the two to return together, the young Jesus leading, with one pierced hand, his bowed and elderly confidant.

The community was managed afterward by a series of elders. The rules of communal living, obedience, and celibacy continued, although increasingly the religious precepts died out. A few years after the leader's death, Edwin M. Stanton, later to be Lincoln's secretary of war, represented in court a man who had been expelled from Economie and who was suing for an accounting of assets and receipt of a just share. Oil and coal had been discovered on the Rappites' land, and at that time many judged the community's worth, which included investment in railroads as well, to be several million dollars! The claim was sustained but an appeal was taken by the society to the Supreme Court, where it was reversed. It was one of many similar suits, all of which were decided in favor of the society.

As the years went on, no new immigrants arrived from Germany, and Japanese laborers were imported to man the factories in the face of a rapidly decreasing population. Around the time of the Civil War a group traveled back to Harmonie and enclosed the old Rappite burial ground with a wall four and a half feet high and a foot thick. The remaining Rappites were all second generation—the grown children of various waves of arrivals from Germany. From birth they had been taught only obedience and none was fit to lead. Funds dwindled. In 1876 only a hundred quaintly dressed elderly men and women walked the cobblestone streets of Economie and the factories were idle. In 1902 there were nine. A photograph taken in about 1915 shows the only two living Rappites—a tiny ancient lady in long skirt and bonnet and a twinkly old man in his cotton jacket and flat hat—posing by the well in Father Rapp's garden. The society was legally dissolved in 1905 after one hundred years of existence. The last member died in 1921.

Today the Great House of Economie is maintained as a museum by the State of Pennsylvania. In Harmonie visitors are shown the sundial, the maze (as restored in 1940), the handsome building designated as dormitory #2 . . . a doorway with a carved rose . . . and a few Rappite houses where several generations of Indiana babies have now been born. A visitor reports that she found a workman improving, with a chisel, the eroded impressions in the rock where once the angel Gabriel alighted, setting one foot slightly ahead of the other.

# 5 UTOPIA REVISITED: ROBERT OWEN AT NEW HARMONY

THERE AREN'T MANY BUYERS interested in purchasing an entire trim little town filled with excellent houses, churches, storehouses, mills, and factories, even when they're surrounded by orchards and fields and parks and gardens . . . to say nothing of the valuable river sweeping gracefully alongside . . . to say nothing of the cheery smell of success wafting over all. It isn't, after all, a very easy item to sell.

When George Rapp put Harmonie up for sale in 1824 he was delighted with the prospective purchaser who read the ad and jumped at the offer. Even the unworldly Rapp, whose life was narrow and whose interests lay heavenward, knew of the famous English idealist and educator, Robert Owen.

Rapp was pleased with the idea of another communal development coming into being on the broad stage set he and his followers had so meticulously constructed. He lowered the price to make the offering more attractive. To Owen, the opportunity to launch the utopian drama that had been developing in his mind for years was irresistible. Rapp and his followers had lived for a decade in Harmonie in expectation of the coming of the Lord and the end of the old order; Owen saw Harmonie as the ideal town in which a new world of his own making could be brought into being.

When Owen and Rapp met to view the property and work out their real estate transaction, Rapp was a white-haired religious patriarch of sixty-seven and Owen an enthusiastic middle-aged atheist of fifty-three—a wealthy industrialist who was internationally famous for the enlightened reforms he had instituted in his cotton mills in New Lanark, Scotland.

Robert Owen had been born in 1771 into the poor household of a Welsh saddle maker and had made his way steadily upwards in the world. He was not a modest man. In later life he related that by the time he was seven the village schoolmaster had no more to teach him. By the age of nine he had completed his formal education and cast off the burden of Christianity, which he found absurd and superstition-ridden. At ten he left home and went to London to work as a draper's apprentice. Although he put in the usual fifteen- or seventeen-hour day in a shop on London Bridge, he found time to read extensively and to write letters to Parliament suggesting changes in the laws. He earned $125 a year and saved almost every penny he had left after paying for food and lodging, because he never in his life seemed to be the slightest bit tempted by costly pleasures, vices, or the frivolous desire for possessions.

Owen had his own yarn-spinning business by the age of eighteen, and two years later, as manager of a mill in Manchester, he joined the local Literary and Philosophical Society where he chatted and debated with young intellectuals and met the poet Samuel Taylor Coleridge. It may have been from Coleridge himself that he first heard talk of utopias in the newly independent country across the sea. Coleridge and a few other young poets had cherished a plan for establishing what they called a "pantisocracy" in the new world. A pantisocracy was, according to Coleridge, the opposite of a democracy. In a democracy, he explained, everyone was dragged down to the level of the lowest savage. In a pantisocracy everyone would be raised up to the level of the most intelligent and aristocratic members. Presumably one simply starts out with enough superior people and the result is inevitable. Coleridge's agent in America found him a piece of land on the Susquehanna River which he guaranteed to be free of indians and roaming herds of bison. But when the poets started squabbling about who was to be elected to go along in this select group the entire scheme fell apart. Is this one of the subjects they spoke about in the Literary and Philosophical Society? Perhaps. It was to be thirty years before Owen would have a chance to establish his own ideal community.

By the age of twenty-eight Owen had accumulated considerable capital and was able to buy, with several wealthy partners, the huge New Lanark mills in Scotland. He also married the former owner's daughter. The Industrial Revolution had begun at the end of the eighteenth century, and as machines took over the work formerly accomplished by human hands, unemployment became a pressing problem. This was particularly true in the booming cotton industry. Inhumane manufacturers were able to increase their production and enlarge their plants and, at the same time, cut wages, since there were so many poor people fighting for employment at any salary. There was also an agricultural depression about the time Owen took over the New Lanark mills, and former farmers flocked to join the urban poor in looking for work in the factories.

The conditions at New Lanark were appalling. Sixteen hundred families and five hundred pauper children who had been hired from the nearby workhouse labored in the mills, living in jammed, unsanitary hovels. The mill children were totally uneducated. Both young people and old brawled, stole from each other, were vicious and violent, drunken and filthy. There were frequent riots. Ignorance and vice brought the improverished workers virtually to the level of wild beasts.

Owen was overcome with distress at the wretched lives of the New Lanark workers, particularly the children, who at the age of five or six were laboring fourteen hours a day in the mills. He raised the minimum working age to ten and reduced the work day to what was then a revolutionary limit of ten and three-quarters hours. He raised wages, installed bathtubs, improved the housing, and saw that all families had fuel, food, and clothing. He opened company stores in which household goods were available at cost. When America's President Jefferson put a temporary embargo on American cotton, all the mills in Britain closed down. Only at New Lanark were the workers paid full wages while the embargo lasted.

One of the most important reforms Owen made was in the field of education. The workers' children entered what was the first nursery school in history at the age of two. Owen had very definite theories of how to teach. He insisted that students were never to be punished—that bad character was not inborn but was the result of unfavorable surroundings. His methods were studied by educators from many countries. Even Grand Duke Nicholas of Russia came to visit New Lanark to see the place where children went to school instead of to work, where the work day was shortened, the wages comparatively high —and production efficient and profitable. Nicholas, who was later to become czar, suggested that Owen come and start a model mill in Russia. Owen declined, but when the grand duke admired the family dessert spoons, which had a Russian emblem on the handle, he gave them to him as a gift. Mrs. Owen was dismayed and it is reported that the butler wept.

Just when Robert Owen began to dream of setting up an ideal community in America is not certain, but when Rapp's town went up for sale, he was ready. He was a restless and romantic man, but he knew how far his money could stretch. To his twenty-two-year-old son, William, he painted a verbal picture of the American Wild West, which neither had seen, and presented a choice: "Shall it be Harmonie or New Lanark?" "Harmonie!" cried the equally romantic William. Mrs. Owen apparently wasn't consulted. Although the four Owen sons and one daughter eventually went to America and settled there permanently,

Mrs. Owen and two daughters remained behind in their comfortable genteel home.

In establishing a community in Indiana, Owen was simply taking the first step in a grandiose utopian plan. He felt that cities and families and all established forms of community life must give way to associations in which five hundred to twelve thousand people would live communally in villages. Each village was to be self-sufficient in agriculture and manufacturing and to be designed in the form of a large quadrangle with gardens in the center and fields outside. The rectangle of buildings would contain housing, schools, lecture and meeting halls, libraries, factories, and all other needed facilities. Children would be taken from their families at age two and housed together in their schools, where they would be taught general reading, writing, arithmetic, advanced science courses, and also several trades as they grew up. Each commune would be governed by its own members. There would be no private property and there would be no middlemen or retailers of any sort. All would share in the labor and its fruits. Owen judged that the work day would not exceed three hours—a happy estimate that has found its way into many other utopian schemes.

Owen planned that the first of these self-sufficient rectangular villages would be built outside Harmonie after a few years of prosperity in the present establishment. It seemed to him, and to many who listened to his flowery impassioned speeches, that success was assured. It was said that, after all, the Rappites were a pretty dull lot intellectually and were fettered by peculiar religious beliefs and an old-fashioned dictatorial leadership, and *they* had made a triumph of the place economically. The new residents were to be modern, enlightened folk, dedicated to new educational methods and progressive ideals. Furthermore, the difficult work of building the town had already been done! Why shouldn't a secular commune work out even more splendidly than its predecessor?

On the ship which brought him to America, Owen discussed his plans day and night with anyone who would listen. He invited all those interested in the new life to join him in Indiana, and displayed a huge painting of his proposed villages. He aired his wish to see the entire world freed of religious belief. Not everyone fancied this sort of talk. His first stop was Washington, D.C., where he called on President Monroe. He told the president and his other visitors—two Choctaw and Chickasaw chiefs—exactly how he planned to save their country from the evils of social and economic inequality. All his life Owen seized any opportunity to expound on his ideas. His father-in-law warned him, "Thou needst to be very right for thou art very positive." Owen was not always right, but he remained positive.

After a stay of eighteen days in Harmonie he left William behind to cope with arrivals, who began appearing in great numbers, and went back east to spread his gospel. He now had a six-foot scale model of the rectangular buildings he proposed for the future, and he predicted, with his usual buoyant optimism, that soon there would be thousands of residents of these towns—the citizens of "the New Moral World." Everywhere he went he urged listeners to join his community. Some of those who came—and people came from every American state and every northern

European country—really *were* dedicated to the ideals of the new order. Others were shiftless ne'er-do-wells, cranks, and crackpots. Some were adventurers and some were embezzlers and some simply derelicts. The town was jammed with people who, for one reason or another, were unhappy in the old society and had come to try the new. And still Owen traveled and talked and advertised in the newspapers, inviting all comers except for "people of color." Owen's philosophy never extended equality to nonwhites, although many of his followers became abolitionists. His suggestion was that Negroes start communes of their own in Africa.

When he returned to the renamed town of New Harmony he also renamed the church. He called it the Hall of New Harmony, to indicate that religion had flown the premises. The plan was to institute for the first two or three years a "Preliminary Society" which would point toward the cause of "the happiness of the entire world." People would supply their own household goods and tools and work for small wages until the time came for a true commune, in which all would contribute their entire holdings and share equally. He closed down the distillery and forbade the sale of liquor, which he always considered a major vice, and instituted three social evenings weekly: one for discussion of community affairs, one for a concert, and one for a dance.

From the beginning the community functioned poorly. There were many intellectuals, but few farmers, mechanics, or laborers. The crops did poorly because the pigs roamed freely and ate the produce. The newly established *New Harmony Gazette* carried articles which spoke of the lack of skillful hands. The vast flour mill, in which the Rappites had turned out sixty barrels a day, was reported idle. So was the sawmill. There were few spinners; no one knew how to run the dye house or the pottery works, nor was there a single citizen expert at making saddles and harnesses. Coopersmiths were nonexistent. There were, however, many candles produced to light the hall for the very popular dances.

Owen returned from one of his frequent trips with a great announcement. A keelboat named *The Philanthropist* was en route from Pittsburgh, carrying more learned people than had ever gathered in one vessel. He dubbed it "the Boatload of Knowledge." In it were educators, geologists, zoologists, and many other scholars of renown—all heading for New Harmony. A French ornithologist had a particularly fruitful voyage. He noted in his booklet that he had spotted on the river "a bald aigle, a blue geai, and le cardinal."

These newly recruited geniuses and eccentrics swelled the population to one thousand. Housing conditions were impossible and families shared tiny dwellings. Mechanics and laborers were in increasingly short supply. One of the Owen sons—all four had now arrived—tried sowing wheat, but his arm ached for two days afterward. Then he joined the girls in the bakery and gamely baked a loaf of bread. When it cooled the bakers gave it to him and suggested that he cut it up into little pieces and use them for bullets. He abandoned such "useful" jobs and took on the editorship of the *Gazette*, which became his career.

Owen decided to design a uniform for the villagers, which consisted of white pants and a short collarless "boy's" jacket for the men and long white pantaloons with a knee-length overslip for the women. He also drew up a new constitution—a job most communitarians particularly enjoy—designating the colony the New Harmony Community of Equality. A visitor wrote that weeds grew higher than the rooftops, pigs and cows and horses roamed freely, the children were wild, and one sunny afternoon he spotted two women having a fist fight! When dinner came the meal consisted entirely of a single tough turkey that someone had shot that day. He said, wryly, that he could not complain of the discomfort of feeling overly full or of having had too much wine to drink while visiting New Harmony.

Another record of inadequate food was left by a schoolgirl who lived, with the other girls, in one of the old Rappite dormitories. She reported that the meals were almost entirely composed of milk and mush and that if ever she escaped from the place she would stuff herself with candies and cakes. Owen, who like many self-made men had developed no luxurious or indulgent habits, announced that he himself ate six cents' worth of food a day, divided into two meals: one taken at 7:00 A.M. and one at 5:00 P.M.

Groups of dissidents began to splinter off and form their own communities nearby. The first of these new settlements was called Macluria and was made up of people who disliked Owen's views on religion. The second had the strange name *Feiba Peveli*. It was formed by one of New Harmony's odd intellectuals—a British architect—who had decided that all towns should be named by a system of his own devising in which the numbers of their latitude and longitude would be translated, code-fashion, into letter equivalents. Anyone seeing the name would then know at once—or after a bit of decoding—the town's exact location. He wanted Owen to rename New Harmony *Ipda Veinul*. When Owen refused, he founded his own place, Feiba Peveli, at 38.11° N, 81.53° W. By his system Washington D.C. would be Feili Nyvul; New York, Otke Notive; London, Lafa Vovutu. The first name represented the latitude, the second the longitude.

There was great disharmony in New Harmony. Much of the dispute centered on the fact that there was still considerable private property, and social equality didn't catch on much faster than economic equality. Many of the educated citizens showed great reluctance to join the labor force and work in the fields or at arduous physical labor. Young women assigned to milk the cows chose to play the piano instead. At the dances girls and boys drew lots and many gently reared young ladies refused to dance with their democratically chosen but uncouth partners. Visitors noted these signs of failure—often with glee.

To the ever enthusiastic Robert Owen, it seemed time for a new ringing proclamation. The fiftieth anniversary of the country was being joyously celebrated on July 4, 1826. Owen declared with great bombast that the year 1776 was the birth of the Declaration of Political Independence and that 1826 was the year of the Declaration of Mental Independence, as shown by life in New Harmony. Few others shared his optimism about the future. One who did wrote a letter to the *Gazette* which said that as new Owenite communes arose throughout the country, names would be needed, and here were a few he'd like to suggest: Peace Glen, Glee, Lovely, Everblest, Philosophy, Olympus, and —inevitably—Utopia.

Six months later the *Gazette* announced defeat and dissolution of the New Harmony Community of Equality. Owen settled accounts—not without squabbling and hard feeling—and he leased land for ten small new communities made up largely of former New Harmony citizens. He went to England and two years later when he returned all had disappeared entirely.

New Harmony was the first nonreligious commune of any duration in this country. Nineteen other communities, also short-lived, had their origins in Owenite theory: twelve in Indiana, one in Tennessee, three in New York, and two in Ohio. New Harmony was the site of the first nursery school in this country, the first coeducational public elementary school, and the first formal adult education courses.

Why did such an idealistic endeavor involving so many talented people fail? The town's music master blamed it on an excess of democracy. "The community was talked to death," he said. Instead of working in the factories and in the fields, everyone sat endlessly at meetings and debates. Most historians share the opinion that Owen was too unselective in opening New Harmony to all who wished to come. One of these wrote, "The cranks killed the colony . . . the selfish, the headstrong, the pugnacious, the unappreciated, the played-out, the idle and the good-for-nothing generally, who, discovering themselves out of place and at a discount in the world as it is, rashly conclude that they are exactly fitted for the world as it ought to be."

The result of this undisciplined conglomeration of associates was not simply dissent but a hopeless gap between theory and action. Vital tasks were never accomplished. Many communes with less lofty principles than Owen's have failed for the same reasons.

The association's famous geologist and educator, William Maclure, for whom Macluria was named, said of the New Harmony experiment, "My experience at New Harmony has given me such a horror at the reformation of grown people that I shudder when I reflect having so many of my friends so near such a desperate undertaking."

Owen, who always stated that his only object in New Harmony had been to procure the greatest amount of happiness for all, continued to write, to speechify, and to try. He had lost almost his entire fortune when New Harmony failed, but he later tried to persuade the governor of Mexico to give him Texas and the province of Coahuila so that he might establish there the renewed New Moral Order. In his old age he was absorbed in spiritualism and spoke frequently to Shelley, Shakespeare, the duke of Wellington, and Napoleon. He collapsed and died on a lecture platform at the age of eighty-seven while discoursing on a favorite subject, "The Human Race Governed Without Punishment."

One of the strangest of the offshoot "Owenite" communes and one which deserves particular mention was Nashoba in Tennessee, founded by a brilliant and bizarre Scottish heiress named Frances Wright. This fiery young woman, who had been orphaned at two and brought up as the ward of leading British intellectuals of the day, was passionately dedicated to the ideal of total sexual and social equality and universal suffrage. She also believed in birth control and free love as essential parts of what nobody then called "women's liberation." As a young woman she was so intimately friendly with the aging General Lafayette that his married children were scandalized. When Lafayette was invited to the United States to the celebration of the fiftieth anniversary of the Declaration of Independence, Frances and her sister Camilla went along with him for the trip. They visited the Rappites in Economie and the Owenites in New Harmony. Frances was a total radical on all issues of political, moral, or religious interest, and she shared Robert Owen's atheism, humane interest in social reform, and advanced views on women's rights.

Her idea for starting her own commune was formulated during this visit and immediately put into action. The land she purchased was a scorpion- and fever-infested two thousand acres, twelve miles from Memphis, Tennessee. She named it Nashoba, the Chickasaw word meaning "wolf." Nashoba was conceived as a commune with one particular social purpose which was, simply, the abolition of slavery. The plan was this: she would buy slaves who would then work on the land and essentially "buy back" their freedom with labor. A percentage of what they earned would, however, be withheld as part of a fund to buy more slaves. The white members of the commune would contribute all their property. It was her grand belief that this system made so much sense that others would imitate it, and soon there would be little Nashobas buying up slaves everywhere and setting them free. Before long there would be no more slavery problem.

Weakened by malaria after the first season, she left Nashoba in charge of one of the white male members (there were never any white women at Nashoba other than the Wright sisters) and convalesced at New Harmony. While there she dabbled in journalism, writing articles for the *Gazette* which promoted free love and birth control as important ideals in communal philosophy. The outside press picked up the news and soon she was notorious throughout the country, and so was her pitiful little commune in Tennessee. Owen, who was already widely vilified for his views on religion and his promotion of a more liberal divorce law, was dragged into the news, and New Harmony was widely denounced as a center of sexual immorality.

Although Frances Wright had planned on little brick houses with piazzas where she and her friends would sit cozily composing tracts about racial equality, the architecture of Nashoba was rat-infested tumbledown shacks. Although her school educated black and white children equally and identically, there were few of either. The former slaves detested the free Negroes who came to live there and quarreling was a major diversion. Miss Wright had laid down a rule which permitted free love between whites, between blacks, and interracially—but only on the basis of mutual consent between the man and the woman. Not everyone accepted this condition and women asked for locks on their doors. Although there were evening lectures—the whites instructing the blacks in the theory of common ownership of property and other such ideals—there were few crops. Camilla almost died of malaria and no little brick houses appeared.

Frances remained spirited. On a trip to England she wore daring Turkish pajamas and rode horses astride and spoke boldly of sexual freedom. She tried to convince the poet Shelley's widow, who was a friend, to join her in her squalid Tennessee paradise. Mrs. Shelley refused. Frances returned and set about the pleasant job of drawing a charter for her "Preliminary Social Community" which was similar to the one written at New Harmony. Both Jefferson and Madison seem to have known of her plan for the gradual abolition of slavery and to have approved it. The fact is, it didn't work. Eventually she tried to sell stock in her community but there were no buyers to be found. When the commune failed she transported her slaves to Haiti where she turned them over to the black president who agreed to let them live there as free men and women. There is no record as to whether this French-speaking republic was the utopia the slaves had in mind.

Frances took to the lecture platform, speaking out all over the United States against the influence of the church in politics, demanding rights for Negroes, women, and the poor. She opposed imprisonment for debt, called for free education for all boys and girls starting at the age of two, and advocated birth control. There were usually threats of arson when a hall was let for her public appearance, but the crowds came to hear and left in a delicious state of shock. She is now regarded as one of the early important figures in the women's suffrage movement and is hailed as the founder of the first women's club, the Minerva Society, which was begun at New Harmony several decades after the great Owenite experiment collapsed.

Owen's sons became leading citizens of the United States. Three of them were married at the same time in a triple wedding ceremony, but the fourth son attracted attention at his wedding by his stand for women's rights. Robert Dale Owen was married without benefit of clergy; he and his wife signed a contract he had drawn up in which he divested himself "now and for the rest of my life" of what he considered the unjust rights which the law bestowed on a husband over his wife's person and property. He continued to live in New Harmony and work for women's legal rights and also for the abolition of slavery as a member of the Indiana Legislature and later of the U.S. Congress. While in Congress he also drafted the bill that established the Smithsonian Institution. He became careless in old age and died ingloriously at eighty-one when he drank a full glass of embalming fluid under the impression that it was mineral water. William Owen was the founder of a repertory acting company named the Thespian Society, which continued in New Harmony for a hundred years. David Dale Owen was a geologist, later appointed U.S. Geologist, who made extensive surveys of the north-western part of the country. Richard Owen was also a noted geologist and a university professor of natural science.

Today New Harmony is still a small town with a population of fewer than twelve hundred. Many of its citizens bear the names of settlers in Owen's community who remained after the dissolution. It is famous for its history as the site of two utopias, and for its Golden Rain Trees, which explode into shimmering bloom every year in June. The first one was brought from Mexico by one of New Harmony's scientists, who planted it in front of his house —the former residence of Father Rapp.

# 6 THE NOBLEST DREAM: BROOK FARM

MEMBER ISAAC HECKER described the Brook Farm community as "the greatest, noblest, bravest dream of New England." The adjectives may seem extravagant and romantic but they precisely echo the heady spirit of Brook Farm. Although the enterprise lasted only six years, no other communal living experiment of the nineteenth century is so well known today. The reasons generally given for its fame are two: the number of remarkable people associated with the community and the high idealism which inspired it. But was that the entire story? What happened at Brook Farm was an explosion of joy, delight, and exaltation. The remarkable thing is that, although communal living is *supposed* to result in great happiness for its members, historically this rarely happens.

Everyone noticed the magical atmosphere. Visitors commented on the cheerful good manners of the men, women, and children. They wrote home about the gay festivities, the animated discussions, the obvious deep satisfaction of the Brook Farmers. Several students at the Brook Farm School wrote memoirs in later years inspired by loving nostalgia which had remained with them throughout life. Aged ladies and gentlemen held reunions in the Adirondacks half a century after the farm was sold. They strolled the woods, picked flowers, sang remembered songs, exchanged stories, and pretended they were back in Roxbury, Massachusetts. No other commune so successfully combined difficult labor, challenging study, and wholesome recreation. No other commune achieved such an idyllic atmosphere.

Several basic differences should be noticed in comparing Brook Farm with New Harmony. Brook Farm was a very much smaller association, which began with twenty members and never exceeded eighty. Most of its men and women were highly educated cultivated folk from the Boston area, many of whom were friends before joining in the association. The result was true social equality and similarity of background which led to common values. A definite and successful effort was made to keep out madmen, paupers, freeloaders, and cranks. Furthermore, although this was not a religious commune, it shared the feature that so closely binds coreligionists. Almost all the people at Brook Farm held the same guiding beliefs and ideals, and that was why they had come. It's true that many of these ideals were a bit fuzzy, but they were cherished with utter sincerity and enthusiasm.

The farm had its origins in a philosophical movement called Transcendentalism. The New England Transcendentalists believed that the world had gone completely astray in the adoration and pursuit of wealth. They wanted a return to simple living, basic crafts, and rural life. They equated contemplation of Nature with worship of God. (All good Transcendentalists spelled "Nature" with a capital *N*.) They took many of their philosophical ideas from the German philosophers who spoke of the nonmaterial world which could be known by intuition and imagination. They spoke of man's ability to "transcend" or go beyond what he could know through his eyes, his ears, and his experiences. The New England Transcendentalists were all university men and many were clergymen and former clergymen who believed that the church needed a new spirit and a new vision. In the Transcendental Club in Boston such seers as Ralph Waldo Emerson, Henry David Thoreau, and Bronson Alcott (the father of the four "Little Women") discussed the philosophical, theological, social, and economic meanings of the new philosophy. Many scoffers, however, tossed around the big word simply as a description of an impractical dreamer. The witty daughter of one philosopher described Transcendentalists as men who "dove into the infinite, soared into the illimitable, and never paid cash"!

One of the members of the Transcendental Club was George Ripley, a disenchanted Unitarian minister who had gone from a rural home to Harvard College, where he graduated first in the class of 1823. For such a man at such a time the route to success was the ministry and Ripley followed the prescribed course. But by the age of forty he was determined to redirect his life in accordance with his new convictions.

There had not been an important secular commune established in the fifteen years since the dissolution of New Harmony and the time was ripe. Transcendentalists spoke incessantly of communal living. Emerson wrote, "We were all a little mad that winter. Not a man of us that did not have a plan for some new Utopia in his pocket."

In the spring of 1841, having resigned his ministry, Ripley and his highly intelligent wife and a group of enthusiastic friends set up their community and applied their excellent minds to realizing their ideals by first learning to milk cows and cultivate the sandy gravelly soil. The farm was a 170-acre dairy farm nine miles from Boston in West Roxbury, now a densely populated urban area, but then a remote rural haven. It had been named Ellis Farm after its former owners who loaned the property but, because of a picturesque winding brook which ran across the property, the newcomers renamed it Brook Farm. It was a charming spot with bosky dells and deep woods and sweet-smelling rolling meadows. They promptly renamed the farmhouse The Hive, because of the exciting bustle and hum. Soon other cottages were constructed and given equally whimsical names.

The community was set up as a joint-stock venture to which all were required to contribute. One of the original members was young Nathaniel Hawthorne, who put down one thousand dollars for two shares. He had laboriously earned the money as a clerk in the Boston Custom House.

Three leading figures in Transcendentalist circles chose not to join the Brook Farm Institute of Agriculture and

Education—formed "to substitute a system of brotherly cooperation for one of selfish competition." Thoreau was to achieve his contemplation of nature without the benefit of a communal setting by spending a solitary two years in a cabin on Walden Pond. Alcott soon started his own ill-fated commune which was tailored to his highly refined tastes and his bizarre taboos against many basic foods. Emerson expressed belief in the theory that the intellectual should also engage in physical labor, but he'd tried it and found that after hoeing he couldn't write. He was happy in his snug house near Concord Bridge. He shared Ripley's disapproval of hired servants and he demonstrated his view by insisting that his two Irish maids sit at the dinner table with him and call him Waldo—much to their agonized embarrassment.

The rules at Brook Farm were few. The idea was to combine simple living and lofty thinking in a classless community. Everyone was to participate in a harmonious routine of joyous work, followed by creative leisure and then by pleasant recreation. Labor would repay the cost of board and all work was of equal value. Ripley hoped to abolish the idea that certain tasks are menial. He felt that if all men and women devoted part of their day to basic physical labor, the working class would be freed of this burden, and all could share the luxury of leisure time for the development of soul and intellect. With the competitive system demolished society would be composed entirely of cultured intelligent equals. Brook Farm was to serve as a model for the rest of the world. Ripley himself performed all tasks with enthusiasm and the exemplary gently reared Mrs. Ripley taught Greek, was overseer of the schoolgirls, wrote musical plays for production at the farm, and ran the kitchen and laundry, where she became particularly adept at ironing pleated nightcaps.

The rest of the Brook Farmers followed their example. Since there were more men than women there was a shortage of help in the kitchen and laundry and young men were conscripted to assist in merry dish-drying and spirited clothes-scrubbing. In the evening after the dishes were polished off, chairs and tables were pushed aside and there was dancing. Emerson noted during a visit that as the young men spun around, clothespins fell from their pockets. Another visitor was enormously amused by "the fanaticism exhibited by well-bred women scrubbing floors and scraping plates and of scholars and gentlemen hoeing potatoes and cleaning out stables, and particularly at the general air of cheerful engrossment apparent throughout."

Not one but three schools were established at Brook Farm: a nursery school for children under six, a primary school for ages six to ten, and a college preparatory school. Classes were held outdoors whenever possible and there were no set drills or study hours. Ripley's reputation as a scholar and a teacher was so strong that soon students about to enter Harvard were sent to him for tutoring. Within a year the fame of the school had spread and young people came from the Philippines, Cuba, and several distant states, as well as from Massachusetts. Although the curriculum centered conventionally enough on Greek, Latin, German, French, philosophy, literature, etc., popular courses were also offered in tree-grafting and other botanical and agricultural subjects. All students worked several hours daily on the farm and in the kitchen. Vocal and instrumental music were studied by everyone, and plays, tableaux, and poetry readings took place frequently— both during school hours and in the evenings when the adults could join both participants and audience. All the schools were coeducational, which was still extremely rare and considered very daring.

Pleasure was pursued with as much inventiveness as work and learning. In addition to dancing, poetry readings, and plays, there were picnics and boating trips on the Charles River in the summer and skating and sledding in winter. In bad weather there were discussion groups with members eagerly voting on the subject for the day. A number of associates were musically gifted and visitors who could perform instrumentally or vocally were assured of an appreciative audience. A visiting troupe of Swiss bell ringers delighted young and old. On some nights groups walked the nine miles or rode in farm wagons to Boston to attend concerts, lectures, and antislavery meetings. Popular amusements which were unanimously disapproved at Brook Farm were hunting and fishing—because they were inhumane—and sedentary games such as cards and chess, because they separated a few people from the group and because they kept you indoors when you could be enjoying Nature.

It was very much the style to express amused contempt for members of the outside world. One would have imagined the novice farmers had been born on the spot. In their literate patter, city people became, with Gallic sarcasm, "the civilisées." People who pursued wealth were held in the greatest scorn. A schoolgirl describing a handsome young man who had just entered her class wrote to her girlfriend in Boston of her horror at discovering that this charming Transcendentalist's father was "entirely absorbed in banks and dollars!"

The young members of the group not only worked at their chores but they thoroughly enjoyed *pretending* to be farm hands and milkmaids. They affected becoming rustic outfits—French-peasant-style blue tunics with wide black belts for the men and short skirts and wide bloomers for the girls. The men grew flowing beards and much longer hair than was currently the style, and the young women defied the convention that would have them pin up their hair in a bun. They wore their locks hanging loose on their shoulders and they fashioned wreaths of wild flowers with which they adorned their hair at picnics and parties. There was a delightful innocence about the farm and the farmers which never changed as the prospects for success dimmed.

A former Brook Farmer who had left his home in Albany, New York, to attend the Brook Farm school as a boy of twelve later wrote about his three happy years in West Roxbury. He recalled with delight the lack of response Brook Farmers accorded to two particularly vehement visiting speakers. The first was a woman who demanded the emancipation of her sex. The Brook Farmers listened politely and then assured the speaker that *their* women enjoyed total equality. If she wished for emancipation they suggested that she come to live with them or start a similar community. The second speaker advocated temperance. He would settle for nothing but total abstinence from the demon rum and he ranted on at great length about the evils of drink. Again the audience was attentive but smug.

There had never been a drop of alcohol consumed at Brook Farm nor had anyone ever imagined there would be.

Brook Farmers were happy to a large degree because they *expected* life, as they were living it, to be happy. As the months passed their crops grew, their schools increased, and the project seemed destined to lead to even greater joy for its members. Hawthorne was the most notable malcontent. Actually, Hawthorne was something of an imposter in this group. His purpose in coming to Brook Farm was not to reform and reorganize society by setting an example of a perfect community. He was not convinced of the importance of living on the land and denying the competitive system. His compelling desire was to write, and his work in the customhouse had left him no time for creative endeavor. He also desperately wished to marry the charming Sophia Peabody, to whom he had already been engaged for some years. It was his hope that at Brook Farm he might labor *and* write, and find in communal living a way of life which would enable him to marry. As the months passed and his days were consumed with feeding livestock and cleaning stables, he found that his chores left him neither the time nor the energy for writing. He was to become one of the few Brook Farmers who would leave in frustration and disappointment. His observations about life on the farm remain in his letters, notebooks, and a thinly disguised fictional account called *The Blithedale Romance*.

Hawthorne's rapid disillusionment with the ideal life is evidenced in his many animated writings. "I like my brethren in affliction very well; and if you could see us sitting around our table at mealtimes before the great kitchen fire, you would call it a cheerful sight," he wrote to Sophia almost immediately upon his arrival. "I intend," he wrote soon after, "to convert myself into a milkmaid this evening, but I pray Heaven that Mr. Ripley may be moved to assign me the kindliest cow in the herd, otherwise I shall perform my duty with fear and trembling." Apparently he was a success. "I have milked a cow!" he wrote, and the letter continued with an amusing story about a stubborn "Transcendentalist heifer." Sophia was kept in intimate touch with his accomplishments. "After breakfast Mr. Ripley put a four-pronged instrument into my hands, which he gave me to understand was called a pitch-fork; and he and Mr. Farley being armed with similar weapons we all three commenced a gallant attack upon a heap of manure."

Two months later his buoyant mood had changed. "It is my opinion, dearest," he wrote, "that a man's soul may be buried and perish under a dung heap or in a furrow of the field, just as well as under a pile of money." Two more months passed. "Even my Custom House experience was not such a thraldom and weariness." And a few weeks afterwards, "Labor is the curse of this world and nobody can meddle with it without becoming proportionably brutified." This was *not* the spirit of Brook Farm.

Hawthorne left but newcomers took his place. The number of sightseers and other visitors became alarming and a fee was instituted for their meals. The feminine guru of the Transcendentalist movement, Margaret Fuller, was frequently in residence. She and Emerson were coeditors of *The Dial*, the official Transcendentalist magazine. Robert Owen came to look around in 1845. He gave two lectures on his socialistic theories and was listened to with interest and respect, although the Brook Farmers deplored the chaos into which New Harmony had deteriorated twenty years earlier. Owen expressed astonishment at the success of Brook Farm and totally denied responsibility for the failure of New Harmony—which shocked his listeners.

Every sort of reformer came to visit and to expound on his views. There was already a "Grahamite" table set up in the dining room for the large number of vegetarians, but followers of Sylvester Graham's currently popular grain and vegetable diet came to proselytize just the same. One food faddist had reduced his diet to bread, maple sugar, and apples. Graham is best remembered today for the graham cracker, but was widely known in his lifetime for his theory that eating animal flesh resulted in unnatural animallike cravings in man. Antislavery speakers came and were made welcome. Advocates of a popular water cure spoke, and the adventurous Brook Farmers gave it a try. The patient lay on the ground while a sluice was opened and thirteen barrels of icy water rushed down an inclined plank and crashed on his back. There is no mention as to whether a cure was effected, but the subject of the experiment reported that he felt as though he'd been pounded by glass balls.

Two notable charlatans caused an uproar of amusement when caught in their deceptions. The first was a man who said he had discovered the secret of going without sleep and had not caught a wink for years. When the Brook Farmers prepared for the night after his evening talk, he naturally declined the hospitality of a bedroom and settled himself in the library with a book from Ripley's excellent collection. A skeptical member of the community awakened at midnight and tiptoed down to the library where he found the visitor snoring in his chair. The second incident involved a vegetarian who claimed to have pared down his diet over the years until he now ate nothing but raw wheat. As the farmers sat down to their meals he smilingly strolled about munching wheat from a bag which he wore at his waist. He aroused considerable curiosity in this group until he was found scavenging in the garbage which was about to be fed to the chickens.

When Brook Farm was two years old another commune was started as an offshoot of the same philosophical movement by one of the strangest members of the original Transcendental Club, Bronson Alcott. Even his friends considered him astonishingly impractical and worried about his seeming inability to support his wife and four young daughters. He was a noted educator, writer, abolitionist, and an avid teetotaler and food faddist. His school, which was denounced in the press but admired by many professional educators, experimented with a number of techniques aimed at self-education and the development of the personality of the child. One of his more radical methods involved punishment of the teacher by the student.

His ideals led him, in 1844, to establish a commune in Harvard, Massachusetts, which he named Fruitlands because fruit was to be the basis of the diet eaten there. Two Englishmen were his partners in this venture. There were never more than fifteen living at Fruitlands, five of whom were children—one English boy and the four Alcott girls. They referred to themselves either as "con-sociates" or "the Family."

Although Alcott shared virtually all of Ripley's ideals, he added a number of principles of his own which made it impossible for him to accept the relative luxury of Brook Farm. For one thing, he not only rejected meat but he also would not permit any animal product to pass his lips. Dairy products were utterly taboo and the consumption of eggs was considered cannibalism. He also eliminated from his diet any foods raised by slave labor such as rice and sugar. Coffee and tea were definitely out because they contained unhealthful drugs. Woollen clothing could not be worn because it deprived the sheep of their coats, and silk was forbidden because worms were sacrificed in its production. Cotton was out because slaves planted and picked the raw material. The Alcott girls were conspicuous in the village school dressed in austere brown linen, the Fruitlands uniform. Reading and writing were accomplished by firelight because it offended Mr. Alcott's refined sensibilities to consider burning the oil derived from a murdered whale.

Although the Alcotts had never enjoyed a life of luxury, the routine at Fruitlands was considerably more stringent that it had been at home. They slept on pallets, arose at dawn, took ice-cold baths, and sat down to a breakfast of mush and water and perhaps a few nuts. Although they intended to eat fruits and vegetables, there were few of either to be had at Fruitlands. Alcott refused to use manure to fertilize his fields because he believed it would transmit animal tendencies to the people who then consumed the crops. Because of his fear of manure in the fields and also because of his conviction that animals were not created to serve man, he kept neither horses nor oxen. An astonished guest asked Mrs. Alcott, who was hard at work making a fire for baking the bread, if there were no beasts of burden at Fruitlands. "Only one woman," was the weary reply.

Because there was no horse to pull and plow, and because there was no fertilizer for the fields, and because Alcott always preferred talking to tilling, the family nearly starved before the venture was concluded. Grain, nuts, and potatoes became their major nourishment, although Alcott had some questions about eating potatoes because they grew underground, hidden from the sun. A farmer who was hired to help the idealists make the farm produce refused to work on a diet of mush and water and was permitted to drink a bit of milk, but when an actual con-so-ciate, a Miss Page, was seen nibbling on a fish tail while visiting a neighbor, she was sent packing. A Brook Farmer of vegetarian inclination who decided to try the life at Fruitlands left hastily when he realized there was no fruit whatsoever. He did, however, bring back impressive tales of the lofty conversation that took place around the almost bare table.

Not surprisingly, a number of extremely odd folk joined the Family. One of these was a nudist. This was a bit much even for the Alcotts, although they respected his ideals in the matter. To avoid offending the Family it was suggested that he walk about naked in the fields during the night, which he did. By day he wore a toga. Another eccentric, who grew an enormously long beard, was harassed by the townspeople and one day four men waylaid him, pinned him to the ground, and attempted to shave him. The man from Fruitlands fought back with a knife, injured several of his attackers, and received a ten-dollar fine. He refused, as a matter of principle, to pay the fine and suffered over a year in jail, much of it in solitary confinement.

Emerson had been urgently invited to join the Family and again declined association. When Alcott wrote an article about Fruitlands in *The Dial*, which spoke mainly of dietary restrictions, Emerson's response had been a single sentence: "We are not yet ripe to be birds." The sage did, however, visit. Discreetly, he left no written comments.

Fall passed into winter and the Englishman, Charles Lane, who had put up the money for the farm, decided to sell out. He and Alcott had frequently visited the Shaker village in Harvard and Lane suddenly decided that he would adopt celibacy for the rest of his life. He did have some concern, however, about the fact that Shakers ate heartily so they they might be strong and able to do the Lord's work. Lane held the view that a man should eat only the barest minimum necessary to sustain life. In any case, within a few months he left the Shakers, returned to England, and was promptly married!

Ten-year-old Louisa May Alcott's diary from the period at Fruitlands is filled with happy jottings about Nature and little poems and pious essays on the pleasures of a vegetarian diet. But near the end of the experiment a poignant cry for rescue appears: "I wish I was rich, I was good, and we were all a happy family this day." Many years later she wrote about the adventure with gentle humor in a newspaper article titled "Transcendental Wild Oats," which was later incorporated in her book *Silver Pitchers*.

Back at Brook Farm life was changing. "The Brook Farm Association of Agriculture and Education" was about to become "The Brook Farm Phalanx." The surplus fruits and vegetables sold at market in Boston were of amazingly good quality, and the school had always been a modest money-maker, but the association was running a small deficit. A great interest in the utopian plans of the French reformer Charles Fourier was spreading across the country and almost forty Fourierist "phalanxes" would be attempted during the next few decades. Three of these would last more than two years and only three others over fifteen months.

The Fourierist plan for communes was popularized in this country by a reformer named Arthur Brisbane, who took what seemed the practical aspect of Fourierism and promoted it—and left behind the nonsense. The nonsense reached fantastic limits. Charles Fourier, who developed a plan for association which was based on what he called "attractive industry," also evolved astonishing theories about the cosmos. The planets, he alleged, had a life form just as humans did. They were born, enjoyed youth, middle age, and old age, and then died. Furthermore, they loved and bred progeny in the form of baby planets. He predicted that in time to come the earth would have six new moons and men would grow tails with eyes on them. This was just *part* of his cosmology. Brisbane also made little of Fourier's interest in free love as an essential part of his system.

Fourier's plans for communities were based on the idea that men are ruled by passionate attractions and that they function harmoniously only when their passions are satisfied by living in communities, known as phalanxes, in which they find their natural vocations in groups and series devoted to certain agricultural and industrial tasks. To achieve a system of "Attractive Industry and Laws of the Harmonies and the Series" involved constructing physical structures to house light industries as well as people. It also required a vast complexity of organization. Brisbane so eloquently promoted the development of Fourierist phalanxes that Horace Greeley gave him space for a column on the subject in his *New York Tribune*. When Brisbane came to talk at Brook Farm, the members were—in a way that now seems unlikely—easily seduced by the notion of becoming the major commune in what was expected to develop into a great new social movement. Brisbane also told the Brook Farmers that they might have the privilege of editing the official Fourierist newspaper, *The Harbinger*. Soon the farmers were divided into Fourierist Groups: garden groups, kitchen groups, waiter groups, hoeing groups, harvesting groups, etc. All the lingo and childish complexity of Fourierist organization was adopted.

In the course of two years as a Fourierist phalanx, Brook Farm plunged step by step directly downward into financial ruin and the noblest dream came to an end. Brisbane had said that eight hundred members and a half a million dollars were needed to start a successful phalanx. Not one of the American phalanxes, and certainly not Brook Farm, was equipped with anything approaching such numbers or such wealth. A large and expensive building was constructed to house the new metalwork and shade and blind industries as well as fill many other functions. On the very day of completion it caught fire and burned to the ground. Putting out *The Harbinger* involved considerable expense. The school was devastated when a young child developed a case of smallpox. Thirty members of the phalanx came down with the disease, and although none of the cases turned out to be severe, anxious parents hastened to withdraw their children.

When dissolution was recognized as inevitable, a young woman at the farm wrote to her best friend, "It is sad to think of the greenhouse plants being sold off. It is sad to see Brook Farm dwindling away, when it need not have been so. . . . With what vitality it has been endowed! How reluctantly it will give up the ghost! . . . I fear the birds can never sing so sweetly to me elsewhere, the flowers never greet me so smilingly. . . . Oh! You must feel with me that none but a Brook Farmer can know how chilling is the cordiality of the world."

Equally reluctant to face the end was a teen-aged boy who wrote in old age of his years at Brook Farm. Here is his description of the finale: "It was as the ice becomes water, and runs silently away. It was as a carriage and traveler fade from sight on the distant road. It was like the apple blossoms dropping from the trees. It was like a thousand and one changing and fading things in Nature. It was not discord, it was music stopped."

# 7 LOVE ONE ANOTHER: THE ONEIDA COMMUNITY

JOHN HUMPHREY NOYES, a twenty-three-year-old graduate of Dartmouth College and the Yale Divinity School, son of a former U.S. Congressman from Vermont and a cousin of an American president-to-be, Rutherford B. Hayes, declared on February 20, 1834 that he was perfect.

He was immediately denounced as a madman, a heretic, a disgrace to his prominent family and his esteemed university. For years there had been wild-eyed prophets stomping about New England and New York proclaiming the coming of Christ, the end of the world, and fifty-seven different varieties of salvation—but *perfection!*

Contrary to all conventional Christian doctrine, Noyes believed that man had been set free from the guilt of original sin. When he broadcast this good news he was, quite promptly, discharged from the ministry. He lost his license to preach and his shocked parishioners in the New Haven Free Church voted him out.

Noyes, who had originally planned a career in the law, had been strongly influenced by enthusiastic revivalist preachers who called their new religion "Perfection-ism." The Perfectionists held that man could attain the state of perfect holiness necessary to salvation. They did not, however, consider sinlessness either a requirement or a possibility. Noyes based his theory of freedom from orig-inal sin on the conviction that the second coming of Christ had occurred eons ago—in the year 70 A.D., to be exact. Since then, he said, men had been relieved of the conse-quences of the fall of Adam and Eve. The world was now a heaven on earth, he preached, and if perfectly clear bibli-cal rules relating to conduct were followed, a state of perfection could almost be considered a certainty.

Those who found his religious views shocking hardly imagined the outrages to come. John Noyes, who like Ann Lee believed that the millennium was NOW, quoted the same scriptural predictions cherished by the venerable Shaker. His interpretation of these passages, however, was completely different. The biblical injunction that in Heaven "they neither marry nor are given in marriage" was taken by Mother Ann, who longed for the celibate life, as evidence that God also prescribed a life of sexual denial. To John Noyes, whose tastes were quite the oppo-site, the passage indicated that all men must love all women, rather than just one mate. To Ann, the command-ment to love one another was God's message of approval of brotherly and sisterly affection. To Noyes it meant that sexual love should be enjoyed with constantly changing partners. The Shakers and the Oneidans agreed completely that the religious life must be based on spiritual rather than material values and that this could only come about when personal property was sacrificed and people lived by sharing. To the Oneidans, however, sharing one's goods and sharing one's body were necessary halves of the same idea. The perfect life of holiness, as realized in Noyes's Oneida Community, was to become the most highly organized and dedicated love-in that the country has ever witnessed.

More than a decade passed from the time Noyes left New Haven until the founding of the Oneida Community. His first step was to return to his home in Putney, Vermont, where he began speaking, writing, and teaching Perfectionism. He made a number of adult converts in his Bible classes, beginning with his sisters and brothers. At this time Noyes began to teach that conventional marriages and their particular obligations and responsibilities would soon cease to be the custom on earth. He wrote to a follower a letter attacking marital love, stating that God willed that husbands and wives share their love with *other* husbands and wives. When the letter was published in a religious magazine many of his startled Perfectionist followers decided to switch to some other leader whose ideas were more digestible.

Despite his attack on the institution, Noyes himself married after a young woman named Harriet Holton enthusiastically accepted his extraordinary proposal. He had written to Harriet, who was already a follower and financial supporter, "We can enter into no engagement with each other which shall limit the range of our affections, as they are limited in matrimonial engagements by the fashion of the world." He wanted it understood that neither should "monopolize" or "enslave" the other's affections, and he said, "I desire and expect my yoke-fellow will love all who love God . . . as freely as if she stood in no particular connection with me." Harriet read the letter and joyously agreed to become his yoke-fellow.

At first Noyes's little group of believers in Putney did not consider themselves a community, but soon eight men and women joined to live together in a system Noyes called "complex marriage." He had written, "In a holy community there is no more reason why sexual intercourse should be restrained by law than why eating and drinking should be—and there is as little occasion for shame in the one as in the other." In 1846 these four couples—the Noyeses, the Craigins, the Skinners, and the Millers—decided to become one family. They signed a document titled "Statement of Principles" in which they named John H. Noyes their "father and overseer whom the Holy Ghost has set over the family thus constituted" and they surrendered "all individual proprietorship of either persons or things" and became "a consolidation of households."

Noyes was ecstatic. He wrote in a magazine, "Separate households, property, exclusiveness have come to an end . . . the Kingdom of God has come." He informed his readers about the holy system of husband-and-wife-swapping. He was promptly accused of adultery by the outraged citizens of Putney and placed, ingloriously, in the town jail. He was released on bond to await trial and when the "family" heard that a mob was threatening violence, they fled, with Noyes in the lead, across the state line to New York.

Soon property was acquired in upstate New York near the town of Oneida. Additional Putneyites joined new converts from other areas and a total of eighty-seven Noyesian Perfectionists formed the Oneida Community. They dedicated themselves to the achievement of self-perfection and the practice of total communalism. In the interests of self-perfection they sought to improve their spirit and intellect by the study of Noyes's religious teachings, by a system of adult education courses, by cultivation of the arts, and by mutual criticism—a primitive group therapy technique. As to their communalism, they lived together as one family, gave up all selfish or possessive ideas and habits—such as exclusive affection for one person—and were free to cohabit with any other member of the family. Rules were established. Either a man or a woman could suggest a get-together, but mutual consent was required. These visits were usually arranged through a third person to verify the consent and also to spare the suitor the possible embarrassment of being directly refused. Many married people joined the community and they were expected to adapt to the social custom of complex marriage. Spouses were to be shared with the community and former husbands and wives were free to refuse invitations from each other. All women at Oneida were known as "Miss."

At first the financial struggle to survive seemed overwhelming. The Oneidans lived in log huts and an abandoned sawmill. They worked the land, preserved fruits and vegetables, which they sold, and tried manufacturing brooms using the broom corn which grew in the fields. Their economic prosperity began when a man who had invented a new type of steel trap joined the community. The deadly trap came in various sizes suited to the capture of every animal from a mouse to a bear. Ironically, the loving Oneidans never objected to the cruelty of the invention. They started manufacturing it at once and it became the best-selling trap on the continent. It remained the community's most profitable industry until silver tableware took first place much later in their history. They also made traveling bags, silk thread, mop handles, rustic seats, and palm-leaf hats.

With the trap business came financial success, and with financial success came new arrivals. Within a few years the population at Oneida exceeded two hundred people and an enormous typically mid-nineteenth-century turreted gothic dwelling was built, which looks today rather like a charmingly landscaped overgrown old resort hotel. It was named Mansion House and the entire happy family dwelled there together under one roof. The house was surrounded by gracious lawns on which the family's favorite game, croquet, was played in all seasons. In winter visitors were amused by the sight of bundled-up men and women wielding mallets on frozen, carefully shoveled and swept ground, surrounded by walls of snow which reached three feet in height. The house itself was pleasantly furnished and steam heated. An attached Children's House provided comfortable quarters for the community's young, who were brought up together as the children of all the members of the community. The possessive attachment of one mother to her child was as sternly disapproved as "special love"—the community's term for exclusive affection between one man and one woman.

Many of the converts were already parents, but there were few new births within the community. Mrs. Noyes had borne five children in the first six years of her marriage, four of whom had died as infants. This was not uncommon at the time, but her husband was so distressed by her pain that he became an early advocate of birth control. He felt that women should be free to enjoy love without the fear of unwanted pregnancies. Furthermore, the community was still shaky financially and it seemed wise to temporarily check the birthrate. Noyes himself instructed the men—young and old—in this matter, which he considered a major masculine responsibility.

In addition to complex marriage there was another unconventional social practice at Oneida. It was called "mutual criticism," and it was the only form of discipline in the community. Anyone with a problem could ask for a criticism, but this was not the only procedure. If someone seemed to need a criticism and made no request the matter was settled without his permission. A frequent problem was that of romance. If a man and woman fell in love they would be severly criticized for lack of correct communal spirit. If the criticism failed the affair would be broken up by separation. The community had opened a branch at Wallingford, Connecticut, and one member would be banished to this faraway post.

In cases of dire offense the criticism would be performed by the entire society, but most commonly a committee of six to twelve people who knew the subject well would participate. As he sat in the center of the ring silently listening and cringing, his friends, one by one, would tell him exactly what they thought of him. They analyzed his character, described his good and bad points—particularly the latter—and listed his disagreeable habits and his improper attitudes. There was to be no spite or nastiness, although all were to speak the whole truth. When each had had his say, the subject usually confessed all his faults, as they had been brought forth in the criticism, and vowed to obey the group's suggestions for self-improvement.

Notes on the sessions of mutual criticism were often written down and printed in the community's newspaper. Noyes himself frequently participated in giving a criticism, and one anguished fellow, remembering the experience, wrote, "I was, metaphorically, held upside down and allowed to drain until all the self-righteousness had dripped out of me." The children were dealt with in gentler fashion, although they had their own mutual criticism sessions in their quarters. One boy, whose case was written up for publication, was criticized for clowning. "It is his delight to divert the boys with clownish wit and he does it to their disadvantage in school and elsewhere." He was commended for his "good heart" and "disposition to improve" and the summing-up of his case included the philosophical observation that "Perhaps there is a place for a clown in such a community as this."

The adults were treated more harshly. One man "was censured for lack of purpose and selfishness in his dealings, for a strong love of dress, for foppishness and pleasure-seeking in social matters, and for the lack of the spirit of improvement and indisposition to qualify himself intellectually to do business properly." Of a woman, the criticism revealed: "She placed a higher appreciation on the intellect and intellectual attainments than on spirituality . . . she does not sufficiently appreciate the profound blessedness of simply loving. . . . It was thought there was a good deal of pride in her character, and that it had never been thoroughly humbled and subdued."

Criticism had several functions. It was intended as a corrective and it was expected to lead to spiritual growth. It was also thought to promote recovery from illness, and in some ailments—which might today be deemed psychosomatic—it seemed particularly effective. It was alleged to be a cure for diphtheria as well. When a number of cases appeared in the community there was cause for serious alarm. Five young people had died. It was decided that all should, as a preventive, eat a more hearty diet, work at deep breathing, and increase their religious faith. If that failed and they came down with the sickness, the course of treatment was "ice and criticism." The ice treatment simply meant that small chips were to be constantly held in the mouth of the sufferer. It is reported that the next fifty-nine cases, which were all treated with ice and criticism, recovered. One poor victim, who received ice but no criticism, died.

The busy Oneidans worked and played with great zest. The women prepared simple meals so that they might have time to work in the shops and leisure for recreation and education. The Mansion House library contained a large number of valuable books on a wide range of subjects. Modern and ancient languages, mathematics, and astronomy were popular subjects of study. There was an orchestra and a choir and a drama group. Along with croquet, baseball was particularly popular. Swimming and boating on the Oneida Lake were enjoyed by adults and by the children. The community also owned hunting land near the lake. When the Wallingford branch opened they purchased some additional recreational property at Short Beach, Connecticut.

Because of their energetic participation in all the activities of the community, the women adopted a distinctive mode of dress. Harriet Noyes set the style by cutting her skirt off at the knees and by clipping her hair just below the ears. Every woman in the family followed suit. The short hair was a symbol of emancipation—from the necessity of attracting a husband and from the hours formerly spent grooming long hair. The short skirts, which allowed ease of movement and were worn over loose trousers of the same material, were extremely shocking over a hundred years ago. Noyes adored them. Although they certainly didn't reveal the shape of the legs, they indicated—for all the world to see—that women indeed had legs. He wrote of the conventional long full skirts: "Woman's dress is a standing lie. It proclaims that she is not a two-legged animal, but something like a churn, standing on casters!"

Visitors came in battalions and stared at the short skirts in horror. The Oneidans greeted them courteously, fed them, entertained them with music, and charged them for their day of amusement. On summer Sundays over a thousand outsiders would visit the grounds. The problem was turned into an asset and the Oneidans began printing ads, offering dinner (sixty cents), dinner with entertainment (seventy-five cents), and a glimpse of their collection of stuffed birds and animals. The visitors gawked, giggled, and joked. A man who had chatted with a member of the family wrote in an account of his visit, "It was somewhat startling to me to hear Miss———speak about her baby!"

Despite their notoriety, the Oneidans lived unmolested for many years. They merrily organized "bees" when major jobs needed doing—husking bees, picking bees, hoeing bees. At bag-making and canning bees, which took place indoors, one member would read aloud to the group from Dickens, Scott, or Austen. They traded goods with the neighboring Indians, who made excellent baskets. They visited the nearby Shakers to watch their religious dances. They invited college glee clubs to come and entertain them. Their own production of Gilbert and Sullivan's *H.M.S. Pinafore* was so successful that they gave many performances in towns in the area. They taught their children reading, writing, arithmetic, languages, science, music, dancing, swimming. They taught them crafts and sent some away to learn new industrial techniques which they could bring back to the community on their return. Several musically gifted girls were sent to New York City for special lessons. Many promising students were packed off to Cornell and Yale.

They were clued in to many of the food fads of the period and they ate meat in careful moderation. They dropped tea, coffee, and tobacco all at one time, and then discovered that everyone missed hot drinks. A spirited experimentation with substitutes began and strawberry-leaf tea and parched-pea coffee were said to be perfectly delicious and highly nutritious. One experiment with "burnt-crust coffee" was a total disaster.

Although their lives followed the dictates of their religion, brief weekday evening discussions of religious principles took the place of prayers. Sundays were not observed as a sabbath but were spent sorting laundry, attending meetings for criticism and the many committee meetings, and playing croquet, picnicking, entertaining visitors. Christmas was hardly noticed and baptism was dropped. The only religious holiday observed was February 20, known as "The High Tide of the Spirit," or simply "The Twentieth." It was the anniversary of the day on which Noyes announced that he was without sin, and it was celebrated with a festive dinner, speeches, dancing, and the exchange of small gifts.

Children lived with their mothers until they were weaned at the age of nine months. They then went to live in a group nursery and later graduated to the Children's House. Mothers were permitted to visit their young whenever they liked, and a number of accounts left by adults who grew up in the Children's House indicate that childhood was a happy time at Oneida. There was sledding on the hill behind Mansion House, skating, swimming, boating, fishing, and jolly companionship. Even the hours spent by the older children making chains for the traps were remembered with amusement. The young were indulged with toys, a playhouse, sports equipment. A crisis occurred when Noyes decided that dolls must be banished. He considered them images and had noted that indeed, the little girls seemed to worship them. He feared that love of dolls distracted children from love of community. One day a large fire was started and the girls walked up, one by one, each tossing her favorite doll into the flames. Adults who watched the cremation reported proudly that their understanding children participated gladly because they had been made aware of the dangers of the "doll-spirit."

At about fourteen, the young people were introduced to the social custom of complex marriage. When it was suggested that early sexual experience stunted the growth of teen-agers, a survey was made with great solemnity, and the claim was refuted. It was found that three-quarters of the young women were taller than their mothers with an average height of five feet four inches and a plump average weight of 136 pounds. The young men were discovered to average five feet nine inches in height and 143 pounds in weight.

The Oneidans loved such statistics. Their newspaper always had new tabulations to report to the community. One issue noted that, despite the small number of births, 161 members were under forty years old and a lesser number—119—were over forty. These facts seem to have been of particular interest to a community in which all curiosity was directed inward. When planned childbearing began, every possible measurement and observation was made to demonstrate the superiority of the crop of new infants.

It was in 1868, after twenty years of careful birth control, that suddenly many of the women of the community began to conceive. This was no random production. Father Noyes had become interested in eugenics. He pointed out that mating was controlled in valuable domestic animals. "Every premium pig tells us what we can do and

what we must do for men," he proclaimed, somewhat un-
poetically. He named his plan for the selective breeding of
human beings "stirpiculture." A group of men and women,
who had been approved by the elders on the stirpiculture
committee, signed a document giving Noyes full power
"in his choice of scientific combinations," and relinquishing
the right to any personal preferences. Of the forty-eight
children born in this experiment, Noyes selected himself to
father ten by different mates. Theodore, his thirty-year-old
son—the one survivor of Harriet's many pregnancies
—was permitted to father three. The other men selected
were allowed one child each.

The sturdy little "stirps" did indeed, as carefully recorded, seem healthier than the general population. Only
one was stillborn and the others seemed remarkably resis-
tant to common early childhood diseases. The entire community doted on them, admired their progress, and paid
careful attention to the latest figures on their growth.

Although the trap business was booming and the Oneida
population growing, by 1873 the community was in serious trouble. Neighbors were infuriated by the Oneidan's
nonobservance of the Sabbath. They loathed their religion,
which they described as "lustfulness made holy." A professor at nearby Hamilton College began an organized cam-
paign to wipe out the community. There was internal discord as well. Noyes was growing old and many considered
him a tyrant. There was no obvious successor. His son
Theodore had no desire to lead the community and had
none of his father's charisma. His next son, by another woman of the community, was also a man of mature years,
but he had been a patient in an insane asylum. Pressures

mounted, threats became more menacing, and in April of 1879 Noyes ran—as he had from Putney—and settled on the Canadian side of Niagara Falls with his steadfast wife Harriet. He never returned to his community again.

With Noyes gone, complex marriage went out of favor. Noyes himself sent a letter from Canada suggesting that the practice be abandoned. The young people—who by his decree had always been paired with older men and women, because of their "superiority in holiness"— yearned for romance and for marriage. Many who had been sent to college came back questioning practices they had formerly accepted, but which, from the vantage point of the outside world, appeared peculiar, embarrassing, immoral. Noyes had left his reluctant son in control. Theodore was one of the community's doctors, a sophisticated graduate of Yale Medical School, who substituted talks on Darwinism for the old discussions of faith. The community resented his leadership.

After Noyes's letter, a great number of marriages took place. But many of the women who hoped to marry the fathers of their children found that their men were already taken. The women who had borne children by Noyes felt particularly abandoned. A generation brought up to believe in the holiness of their lives felt shamed by the reversal of policy. With many of the children now "legitimized," the husbandless women realized that if they reentered the outside world they would be considered depraved and their children bastards.

When the community was reorganized into a conglomeration of husbands and wives, communal sharing of property no longer seemed practical. The Oneida Community became a joint-stock company known as The Oneida Community, Limited. Stock was fairly distributed according to the number of years members had spent in the community. Children were guaranteed $80 to $120 a year and eight months' schooling until the age of sixteen, when they were to be given $200 to assist them in making the transition to self-support. Some members stayed on and others ventured out into the world, asking that the dividends on their Oneida stock be sent to them in plain brown envelopes so that their postmen and neighbors would not recognize this evidence of a scandalously unconventional past.

The Oneida Community, after thirty-two years of association, became transformed into a successful and enlightened capitalistic enterprise. Today Oneida is a leading producer of stainless steel and silver-plated tableware, with over three thousand employees. Mansion House has been divided into apartments and the children of descendants and outsiders still sled on its hill and play on the gracious lawns.

Oneida is remembered today as the most daring of the long-lived utopian communes. Some remember it for one of its members, Charles Guiteau, who lived in the community as a young man, left to go into politics, and unsuccessfully sought appointment in President Garfield's administration. In 1881, as the president was boarding a train in the Washington railroad station to deliver a commencement address at Williams College, Guiteau—in obedience to the voices of new gods—shot him in the back. Garfield died of his wounds after six weeks of great suffering, and Guiteau was hanged.

Oneida is remembered with the greatest interest for its

extraordinary founder and leader, whose ability to inspire faith in others was the strongest single factor in its long history. In the book he wrote in his later years, *A History of American Socialisms*, Noyes modestly mentioned his community last, singling it out primarily as the only religious community of strictly American origin.

One of Noyes's sons, Pierrepont Noyes, wrote a book about his father in the 1930s called *My Father's House*. Pierrepont was one of the children born of the stirpiculture experiment, and after Noyes's flight the teen-ager visited him in Canada. He records the judgment of the aged deaf patriarch set down in a letter written when Oneida became a joint-stock company. Noyes wrote, "We made a raid into an unknown country, charted it, and returned without the loss of a man, woman or child."

Pierrepont read the letter in awe. "Could anything be more dramatic," he exulted, "than a man now in his seventieth year, standing amid the ruins of his lifework shouting 'Victory!' "

# 8

## A SPIRITUALIST AND A REVOLUTIONARY: BROCTON AND ICARIA

SURELY ONE of the most bizarre of all nineteenth-century communities was that of the Brotherhood of the New Life, also known, because of its location in Brocton, New York, as the Brocton Community. It was preceded by a less successful experiment, the Mountain Cove Community in Virginia. The mystical religion to which the brotherhood was dedicated had been dreamed up, written about, and widely promoted by its leader, priest, and dictator— Thomas Lake Harris, the most famous American spiritualist of his day.

Spiritualism enjoyed a great vogue in the second half of the nineteenth century. Although many ancient cultures practiced some form of communication with spirits of the dead, the subject was scarcely mentioned in Europe after the Middle Ages. The revival of interest in ghostly matters started up suddenly, spread throughout this country and Europe, and has never totally died out since. The wish to speak again with loved ones who have died, to seek their advice, to be assured that they are happy in the other world is so widespread that anyone claiming ability to arrange such interviews will probably always find customers.

The so-called Modern Spiritualism caught fire when two sisters, Kate and Margaret Fox, began to hear strange rappings at night. The year was 1848 and the girls lived with their parents on a farm in New York. It seems that they had—of all things—made contact with the spirit of a man who told them that he had been murdered in their house. He spoke to them in a code they worked out together in which various numbers and combinations of raps could be used to answer questions. When the Fox sisters went to live with their older sister whose home was in Rochester, sure enough—they were able to contact their spirit there as well. Soon these "Rochester Rappings" made newspaper headlines. The sisters were famous. They toured the United States and England as mediums who brought people into contact with the spirits of former friends and relatives. In no time at all other mediums with the gift for ghostly communication were announcing themselves, and being accepted and sought after by an avid public. Even the sober Shakers heard from spirits of the dead during this period and they left many detailed accounts of their communications with Mother Ann and other notables from the world beyond.

Much later Margaret Fox publicly confessed that it had

all been a hoax and that the "raps" heard by their audiences were sounds that she and Kate produced by cracking their toe joints. By this time mediums were everywhere, spiritualist associations were publishing journals, and no one seemed to feel that this admission discredited anything or anyone—except perhaps Margaret and Kate. Anyhow, a bit later, Margaret took it all back and said that they really *did* talk to spirits, and although some folks were skeptical, many felt that this certainly didn't indicate that *others* weren't doing a fine honest piece of work in the spiritualist business.

Thomas Lake Harris came into adulthood in this atmosphere, and he was not particularly surprised when certain rapping spirits informed him, in 1851, that they had located the Garden of Eden—the exact spot where Adam and Eve had last trod. No one, said the spirits, had walked there since. Although most people, if asked, might have guessed that the Garden of Eden was in a more easterly part of the world, the spirits had announced that it was in —surprise!—Mountain Cove, Virginia. Harris, a former Universalist preacher who had become a mystic and medium, received the message from the spirits and issued a general invitation to join in establishing a community in Mountain Cove. "You are the chosen," the letter said. "Lead in the conquest." What Harris had learned was that Jesus would return to earth on this spot. Although many of those chosen happily pitched in with all the funds at their command, two years passed and no one saw Jesus. Furthermore, the commune was bankrupt. Everything came to a crashing close with unseemly arguments about property and money and other such unspiritual matters.

After this fiasco Harris went off to England, where he discussed his mystical-religious theories before admiring audiences. On his return he married a woman who, like her husband, sincerely believed in angels, demons, and fairies. In addition to acquiring a wife, Harris also acquired a sponsor and companion in the person of Jane Warring, a wealthy socialite who had left her scandalized family to follow Harris. Mrs. Harris not only put up with Miss Warring's constant presence, but she also shared her husband with his invisible heavenly "counterpart" whose name, he said, was Queen Lilly of the Conjugal Angels and whose nearness he felt at all times. He spoke with her in trances and many of his commands were simply orders which he received from this spiritual companion. As the result of their communications and financial donations from Jane Warring and Laurence Oliphant, a British diplomat, adventurer, novelist, and member of Parliament, Harris set up a spiritualist commune in New York on the south shore of Lake Erie.

Sixty adults and children made up the population of the new community. A local newspaper of the time reported the group as including "five orthodox clergymen; several representatives from Japan; several American ladies of high social position and exquisite culture." The twenty Japanese had been brought to the commune by its most distinguished member, Laurence Oliphant. They were all members of the Samurai class and Oliphant considered them excellent subjects for Harris's teaching because of certain similarities between their belief in a "divine mother" and Harris's belief in his heavenly Queen Lilly. Strange as it may seem—and it certainly rocked the Houses of

Parliament—Oliphant believed Harris's claim that he was a deity. He also believed that salvation lay in submitting himself completely to this strange American's will.

There is still considerable mystery surrounding the person of Laurence Oliphant. Born into a wealthy and cultured family, he was an attractive intelligent man who was also noted as a social charmer and ladies' man. Before his election to the House of Commons he served as secretary to Lord Elgin, war correspondent to the *London Times*, and first secretary to the British delegation to Japan. He wrote a number of books, the best known of which told of his travels to Russia and Nepal and was called *Episodes in a Life of Adventure*.

Oliphant, who along with both his father and mother had long shown some interest in religious mysticism, had met Harris in London. He applied for permission to join the new spiritualist commune and contributed a large amount of money, which enabled Harris to obtain the property. After some delay, Harris sent his permission to Oliphant, who immediately departed with his mother— his father had recently died—for the farm in New York. Harris assured his benefactors that they were there on probation. He sent Oliphant to live in solitude in a hut away from the other members of the community and assigned him the most unpleasant chores. Lady Oliphant was given kitchen duty and mending.

The Harris-Oliphant relationship was that of a god and a totally submissive subject. The god was Harris, who believed that he was a divine being, reigning jointly with his spiritual counterpart, Queen Lilly. The subject was Oliphant who, for complex psychological reasons, was overwhelmed with a need for self-humiliation and self-abasement. He wrote of Harris: "I gave him my all until I had no personal clinging left. . . . He has crushed out to a great extent personal desire, thereby making my will more elastic to God's touch."

The talk among Oliphant's friends in London was that he had simply become insane. Others said he was half-dead of syphilis after his years of sexual indiscretion and that he felt Harris could cure him. Harris certainly believed that he was capable of effecting cures and both rumors may well have been true.

Harris's religious doctrine was based on a belief that "all life, and with it the virtues and energies of life, are the result of divine inflowing." He believed that God, in making man in his likeness, breathed life into him, creating a channel through which man was constantly bathed in heavenly breezes—until the fall. Since then the connection between man and God had been severed, and Harris felt he had to restore it. He believed in fairies and demons and he spoke frequently with both as well as with a long list of spirits. He had perfected "internal respiration" in himself and he announced to those who turned over their money that their bodies and their will, through a vow of total obedience, might also hope to regain contact with the divine breath. Some members of the commune soon became convinced that they had attained this desired state.

A newspaper article about the new community with the headline "Will It Succeed?" concluded with the opinion that it would. "Communities based upon peculiar religious views have generally succeeded," the reporter blandly observed, pointing out the experience of the Shakers and the Oneidans.

Harris also believed in a bisexual God who had manifested the masculine aspect of his being in him and the feminine in the mysterious Queen Lilly. He assigned fanciful names to the communitarians, which had been revealed to him by Queen Lilly while he was in a trance. He was Faithful; Oliphant was Woodbine; Jane Warring was Dovie. Faithful and Dovie and the neglected Mrs. Harris lived in a thirty-room mansion, strode about gowned in silks, smoked pipes, and dined luxuriously. Water had been piped in from two miles away for a fishpond. Scandals swept the neighborhood when it was discovered that Harris urged the women of the community to seek contact with their spiritual mother, Queen Lilly, by lying in bed with him at night. Apparently Queen Lilly resided within him and this was the only sure method of achieving contact.

The other members of the commune were denied smoking and all forms of physical luxury. They were issued commands and punishments at Harris's will. After two years Oliphant was still kept in virtual isolation from the other members of the community. A restaurant was opened at the property's juncture with a small railroad station and he was ordered to enter the trains at the stop and peddle fruit from the community's orchard. He had not been permitted to speak to his mother during the two years, although he watched her from a window. He cleaned the stables, curried the horses, polished boots, worked for ten hours at a stretch in the vineyard. When friends implored him to return to England and to Parliament he wrote, "My states are not advanced enough," and he signed himself *Woodbine*.

Years passed and Oliphant returned briefly to Europe. When he came back to Brocton he brought a wife. Alice Oliphant was as willing to offer Harris her submission and her property as her husband had been, and they obeyed when Harris decreed that they not consummate their marriage. Alice lived in the mansion with Harris, Mrs. Harris, Miss Warring, and several other selected women. Oliphant stayed in his shed. When Harris decided to open a second commune in California, where the climate pleased him, he took Alice along and left her husband behind. In California Harris raised grapes and wrote long poems and strange rambling prose works about "The Lord, the Two-in-One-Chrysantheus-Chrysantheo, Christus-Christa."

It was not until fourteen years after Oliphant submitted to Harris's will that the rupture occurred. Oliphant, who had not been permitted to see his wife for years, suddenly began to hear from *his* spiritual counterpart, whom Harris had named Alawenie. Alawenie said that he, Laurence Oliphant, was now favored by certain influential angels, who had deposed Harris because he was ruled by a consuming love of money and power. Oliphant denounced Harris and successfully sued for the return of a portion of his financial contribution to the community. Alice defied Harris's will by leaving the community and, after a brief period of teaching poor children in southern California, she rejoined her husband, who had returned to England alone. Oliphant wrote: "Only a man who has suffered my bondage could know, by contrast, my splendid sense of liberty." He dashed off a number of impenetrable mystical-religious books of his own. Later he became obsessed with a mission to promote Jewish recolonization of Palestine. He and Alice went to live in Haifa, where Alice died. Her spiritual presence remained with him, however. Five months before his death he married Rosamond Owen, Robert Owen's granddaughter, who assured him that Alice had communicated to her that she wished this union to take place.

Harris, in California, became caught up in what seems a rather early manifestation of West Coast youth-cultism, and as he himself grew old he insisted that he was more vigorous physically and mentally than he had been as a young man. He also announced that the wine he was so profitably making was imbued with the divine breath. This may or may not have promoted sales. He renamed himself King Chrysantheus, renamed the months Love, Peace, Dove, Adoration, etc., and decided that in his present utopia of the West all marriages were null and void each January 1 and everyone could switch partners. It was charged that nude bathing, group sex, and unspeakable degeneracy ruled the community. Eventually he sold out at a fine profit and invested in real estate in Florida. For a man so incessantly preoccupied with spirits, Harris always retained a firm grip on the value of money. In his last years he gave up all the fancy names and took to calling himself —very simply—God. He continued fighting against devils, speaking to angels, communing with spirits. He died at eighty-three in 1906. The remaining faithful hoped, watched, and waited for three days, in expectation of his resurrection. Although, as one of them wrote, they "did not recognize the event as death," his body was dispatched to the crematorium and twelve followers held a simple service in praise of their deity.

In analyzing the history of the communal movement most authorities agree that a set of shared religious convictions is the one necessary ingredient for success. Durable sectarian communities—the Shakers, Ephratans, Oneidans, Hutterites, Amanans—contrasted with short-lived secular experiments such as New Harmony and Brook Farm, seem to prove the point. Those who wish to refute this theory most frequently point to Icaria as an example of a purely secular commune that *did* succeed. Icaria, after all, lasted for half a century—didn't it?

Well, more or less. No communal experiment persevered for so many decades despite what would seem to be devastating problems. Whether this can be considered "success" is hard to say. Life in Icaria was a perpetual battle. The Icarians were tragically beset by hardship, lucklessness, and a continuous seething and boiling disunity. In theory they were all for community. But even when things were going along relatively easily these French rebels simply could not resist arguing, splitting into warring factions, and plotting against one another.

Icaria was an imaginary peaceful never-never land which was transformed into a grim embattled reality. The settlement was directly inspired by a utopian novel written by a French political idealist named Etienne Cabet.

Cabet was a born conspirator and an active member of one rebel faction after another. When French King Louis Philippe appointed him attorney general to Corsica—then under French rule—the idea was really to get the trouble-maker out of France. His radicalism, however, cost him his position and he returned to France. After engaging in further revolutionary activity, he was banished from the country for five years. He went to Belgium, from which he was also expelled, and he continued on to England, where he sat out his period of exile writing a history of the French Revolution.

He also wrote another book *Le Voyage en Icarie*—a utopian novel about a make-believe land named Icaria where people lived in peace and prosperity, having abolished monarchs, class distinctions, unfair taxes, and other impediments to the happiness of mankind. In Icaria majority rule dictated national policy and the vote was extended to all men, although Cabet was not quite radical enough to grant it to women. All citizens shared equally in the products of agriculture and industry. Actually, Icaria was a pretty ordinary sort of utopia, owing a considerable debt to Sir Thomas More's *Utopia*, with which Cabet was thoroughly familiar.

When Cabet returned to France the book became a best seller. Like most utopian proposals, it was not only a plan for good government but an implied criticism of the present political and social order, and this made the book enormously popular in an age of revolutionary fervor. The government, the clergy, and the police increased its readership by opposing it. By 1847 there were thousands of social reformers from France, Switzerland, Spain, Germany, and England who referred to themselves as "Icarian Communists." When and where, they asked and urged, would Icaria be established, so that they might go to live there?

Cabet rushed back to England in great excitement to

visit Robert Owen, who was always delighted to chat about utopias, even those that didn't conform to his own cherished philosophy. Owen was, at this time, an elderly man of seventy-six, much absorbed in spiritualism. He had, not long before, attempted without success to acquire property in Texas where he hoped to make another attempt at establishing his own version of Utopia. He had never seen Texas but he knew it was wide and open. In 1846 Texas had been admitted to the union and the new state was making positive attempts to attract immigrants. Texas, the Englishman assured the Frenchman, was truly paradise—the only, the perfect, the obvious site for Utopia, or whatever you called it. *Icaria?*

*"Travailleurs, allons en Icarie!"* Cabet announced in the radical press. *"C'est au* Texas!" Cabet had contracted to buy, from an American land agent, a million acres bordering the Red River in east Texas. The price seemed fantastically low, and financial contributions flowed from thousands of would-be Icarians.

At just about the time when Brook Farm was closing down and the Oneida Community was being established, an advance party of sixty-nine political radicals—all strong young men selected to brave the first hardships—departed Le Havre to lay claim to Icaria. Their plan was to begin erecting dwellings for the expected eventual arrival of up to a million Icarians! They stood on the deck of the ship shouting, *"Partons pour Icarie"* in noble enthusiasm to their supporters, who chanted *"Au revoir"* over and over again from the dock.

Before the ship reached New Orleans, great political changes took place in France and the Republic was proclaimed. Cabet himself, who had not accompanied the advance party, was one of the men being considered for the presidency. Some members of the group wished to return at once. Icaria, they said, could now be established right at home—in a new France. The majority ruled against it, however, and the trek to Utopia began, although a few dissidents did return to France. The settlers had been assured by the land agent that they could simply float by barge up the Mississippi and the Red River from New Orleans to their property, but this was not so. Great barriers of trees, which had washed down the river in floods, blocked their passage, and the last 250 miles from Shreveport became a nightmare trek through swamps and uncharted forests. Their food was inadequate, their ox carts broke down, their doctor went hopelessly mad just as malaria struck.

When the sorry crew reached Icaria they found not a million but one hundred thousand acres. Furthermore, the area was laid out like a checkerboard, with every other square retained by the state of Texas for future sale and development. Each square plot touched others only at the corners. Even these plots could only be claimed if a log cabin was erected on each one within a few months. The hapless Icarians had been unscrupulously duped. They set to work frantically and an urgent summons for help went out to Cabet in France, as men began to drop from malaria and others quit the venture and made their way back to New Orleans to look for employment. When the reinforcements arrived they numbered a mere nineteen, and after evaluating the inaccessible and infertile acreage, a decision was made to abandon the property, leave Texas, and search for Icaria in a friendlier spot. When Cabet and several hundred fellow adventurers joined them in New Orleans, disagreements of one sort and another resulted in the departure for France of about a third of their number.

Cabet learned that the former Mormon settlement in Nauvoo, Illinois, was up for sale, and knowing of Robert Owen's purchase of Harmonie from the Rappites, he understood the advantages of stepping into a ready-made utopia. Two hundred and eighty Icarians made the trip to Illinois, singing of equality and brotherhood as they marched. Twenty died of cholera en route. With typical Icarian bad luck, the Mormon temple, which they planned to restore as a recreational center, was almost immediately destroyed by a tornado. Also, alas, the Icarians were not born agriculturists any more than the Brook Farmers had been, and they found the care of crops and farm animals a bit trickier than they'd imagined. But enthusiastic members in France continued to support them with financial donations and the future looked promising. They started a school, a newspaper, a little theater group, and a fifty-piece orchestra. Life was beginning to seem really quite—well, Icarian.

A major error was made almost immediately. Instead of accepting Nauvoo as a permanent home, talk of the "real" Icaria began to bubble and boil. After all, the location was supposed to have been selected for some ideal reason—not just because a village happened to be available. Inspiration led a small search party to Iowa, and acreage in the southwest part of the state was purchased for future settlement, with a very large mortgage and considerable optimism.

In Nauvoo life was simply too peaceful for its spirited

residents. Cabet began playing politics again. His people had agreed to accept him as a dictator for the first ten years, but he had relinquished this honor and instituted a more democratic board of directors. Apparently he changed his mind. When three directors he disapproved of were voted in he refused to accept them. Factions were formed, pro-Cabet and anti-Cabet. When actual rioting broke out, the old man himself—he was now in his late sixties—leaned from his library window and called out to his supporters to rally round and capture the assembly hall! Dishes were thrown, Icarians struck out at each other with sticks and stones, a schoolmistress was dragged by her hair from the school as her students wept. The scene was about as unutopian as can be imagined. When the dust settled and the broken glass was swept up, Cabet—the once-revered leader—was expelled from the Garden of Eden with a relatively small band of loyal men and women. They left for St. Louis where Cabet, worn by the struggle to bring life to a dream, died of a stroke.

After their idol's death his followers lived and worked in St. Louis for a while, gave up smoking in honor of his memory—he had tried to enforce this prohibition in Nauvoo—and sent their children to the public schools to become Americanized. Later they established a small commune which was recognized in France as the only true Icaria and which received the available financial support. After a short period of peace, dissension flared and the venture ended in shouts, accusations, hostility, and more broken crockery.

Back in Nauvoo, contributions from abroad had ceased with Cabet's eviction. The body, deprived of its head, was about to collapse. Interest in Icaria died out in France and very few new arrivals joined the original group. Debts on the land in Illinois, when added to payments on the property in Iowa, became clearly impossible to manage, and the diminished group of Nauvooans sold out and moved on to Iowa, where they constructed wretched sod huts in which they proceeded to starve. By 1863 there were only thirty-five Icarians still persevering in this almost uninhabited area of the country, but during the Civil War their flocks and farm produce increased in value and they were able to avoid financial disaster. Membership grew to seventy-five and they met again in their central assembly hall for spirited singing and debating, for musical evenings, and for theatrical performances. Over the entrance a large sign read: EQUALITY–LIBERTY 1776–1876. With the passage of years, reverence for the leader had returned, and passages from Cabet's writings were read aloud after dinner and fervently discussed.

Suddenly there were arguments. Some Icarians wanted to expand the facilities; others wanted to consolidate their position, move slowly, and admit no new members. One party wanted to amend the constitution; the other responded by drawing up terms for separation and division of holdings. The discord became so intense that they took the case to the Adams County Court of Iowa. It was decided that since the community had been incorporated as an agricultural group it had exceeded its rights by engaging in a bit of manufacturing. The old charter was canceled and a division of property made. Two new communities were founded. The separatists took the old name—Icarian Community—and stayed on the same site. The older members, who had held a conservative view, settled only a mile southeast and called their establishment the New Icarian Community. The separatists nobly rushed to grant their women the vote. Next they abolished the presidency in favor of a four-member trusteeship. But they were unable to meet their debts and they soon fled their creditors. A few diehard members opened a new commune in California which lasted only a short time. Others tried to join the New Icarian Community, but were adamantly refused admission.

The New Icarians held on until the turn of the century. Then the little group of survivors divided their communal assets equally so that they might each have a bit of property to pass on to their children, who thought brotherhood and equality and liberty were all grand ideals—but who had not the slightest interest in living in Utopia.

# 9 THE SONG GOES ON: THE CONTEMPORARY SCENE

THERE WERE, of course, many, many others. New styles of success were attempted and new variations on the theme of failure frequently resulted. Intercommunal warfare hit a peak when Eric Janson, leader of the Swedish Bishop Hill community in Illinois, was fatally shot in a courthouse by a former follower who had brought suit against him and who suddenly lost patience with the orderly slowness of the trial. A new type of experiment floundered when the anarchist community on Long Island named Modern Times—which tolerated all comers—began to attract polygamists, nudists, a strange lady who starved herself to death, and a bevy of gangsters from New York City, who found it a hospitable hangout. Adventist colonies were founded and the Mormons made a second attempt at communalism, which lasted for a decade, until it was abandoned because of growing dissatisfaction of the members.

But in the decades after the Civil War, land became more expensive, small-scale farming proved less and less profitable, and the cottage crafts made by communitarians were unable to compete with the products of industry. The rural and small-town poor, who had always been candidates for religious communes, were moving to the cities. Sophisticated urban reformers were disillusioned by the failure of back-to-the-land secular experiments and were trying new ways of protesting social wrong. The saga of the communal movement went into a long recess, punctuated by a few scattered happenings.

In 1886 an American engineer conceived a grandiose scheme for a community of several million to be located on the Atlantic coast of Mexico. Called Topalabampo, it attracted four hundred Americans who labored for several years before lack of money and drinking water, and the Mexican government's change of mind, brought the project to an end.

In the 1890s several communes directly inspired by Edward Bellamy's *Looking Backward* rose and fell. The so-called Women's Commonwealth, whose members referred to themselves as Sanctified Sisters, had chapters for some years in Texas and Washington, D.C. In New Mexico a community named Shalam was dedicated to the care of orphaned children. The children were taught the evils of liquor, the benefits of a vegetarian diet, and the wonders of spiritualism. California's Llano Community had, in 1917, one of the first Montessori schools in the country.

Communal living, which had been predominantly an east coast movement, caught on in the west, and many of the California communes of the late nineteenth and early twentieth century were quite as strange as the most far-out communes in California today. The Universal Brotherhood at Point Loma was established by a theosophist and student of the occult who called herself the Purple Mother and who dressed her male followers in military uniform. The community's temples had vivid aquamarine and amethyst glass domes. Five hundred people lived at Point Loma in 1907—its peak year—and their "Raja Yoga" school taught believers' children the spiritual, mental, and physical balance which would enable the soul to progress upward in later incarnations.

The Kaweah Community required applicants for admission to name all the books they'd read in the past year and supplied a reading list for those who were found wanting. Members, according to one of them, included "dress reform cranks, phonetic spelling fanatics . . . uncooked food believers. It was a mad, mad world, and being so small its madness was the more visible." The Kaweahans picnicked in the redwood forests, named the largest specimens after socialist gods, and were photographed for posterity in front of the Karl Marx Tree.

The members of the Association of Brotherly Co-operators lived on an "endenic" diet which forbade any cooked foods and permitted only grains and fruit and nuts. They moistened raw ground wheat and oats with fruit juice and referred to their delicacies as "live food," since they believed that contact with fire removed food's "vitality." Another California commune was established by a group of intellectual Poles, who had read about Brook Farm in Cracow! Count Charles Bozenta Chlapowski; his actress wife, Helena Modjeska; and a number of friends sailed to New York, took a train to Washington to pick up some farming manuals from the Department of Agriculture, and boarded a steamer for Los Angeles. When their crops failed and their animals died, one of their members sat down and wrote the novel *Quo Vadis* and most of the others went home. Madam Modjeska became a huge success on the American stage, acting with such leading men as Edwin Booth and Otis Skinner.

The Koreshans—who were first-rank oddities—had their own view of the cosmos, which had nothing to do with any recognized branch of science. They insisted that the universe was a ball, and that we are living on the *inside* along with the sun, moon, and stars.

Two of the old German sectarian groups entered the twentieth century in a state of perfect preservation. The Amanans had eight prosperous villages in Iowa, protected their children from any learning other than religion and simple arithmetic, and attended church services eleven times weekly. In 1932 they followed the example of the Oneida Community and became a joint-stock company. They are now major producers of home freezers.

Only the Hutterites still live as they did a century ago. This pacifist religious sect, which migrated to America in the nineteenth century, has colonies in South Dakota, Montana, Minnesota, Washington, and parts of western Canada. Life is austere in the Hutterite communities, where newspapers, magazines, radios, television sets, automobiles, and even indoor plumbing are scorned. Adults and children still dress in the quaint clothing of a century ago. Although a number of young men take off for the outside world every year, most return after a short spree to the isolated security of their communities.

The earliest commune that can be linked to the modern revival is Koinonia Farm near Americus, Georgia, not far from the Civil War prison town of Andersonville. Situated in Ku Klux Klan territory, this interracial commune has been in existence since 1942, when it was established by an idealist named Clarence Jordan as a place where blacks and whites could live and work together. Koinonia—the word is Greek and means "togetherness"—is at this time the home of thirty-five communitarians, most of them Southerners, who range in age from their teens to their seventies. They have survived periods of crude and violent harassment from the Klan, particularly during the fifties. The community mail-orders pecans, fruit cakes, and candies all over the country, and also markets farm produce, timber, and cattle. Profits are put into a charitable fund used for various enlightened purposes. Like Brook Farm, Nashoba, the Owenite and Fourierist communes, and the five-year-old Twin Oaks Commune in Virginia, Koinonia was designed with the purpose and expectation of inspiring many imitators. In this respect alone it has proved disappointing.

A lively book about the old communes written in 1959 by Everett Webber ended with the announcement that there was no possibility of a resurgence of rural communal living. "The song is done," was the author's conclusion. Eight years later the revival was off to an explosive start. The search for Utopia had begun again.

The movement officially took off in the late sixties when the center of hippiedom, the Haight-Ashbury section of San Francisco, began to empty out. The overpublicized, overcrowded, and increasingly crime- and disease-ridden area had become uninhabitable, and the cry that went out was "Back to the land!" The idea seemed strikingly original to most who heard it, and hordes of young people enthusiastically fanned out to the ranches, farms, hills, and mesas of New Mexico and California. In the first years, the revived interest in rural communal living was almost exclusively a West Coast youth movement. Its members were refugees from urban centers or young people who arrived as drop-outs or graduates of high schools and colleges who sidestepped the urban phase of hippie life entirely. Today the movement has spread across the country and increasing numbers of communitarians in their late twenties and thirties have brought along the kiddies and joined experiments in collective living. These adults have also dropped out. Instead of leaving schools, they have voluntarily fled urban pressures, commuting, mortgages, bosses, pollution, and the forty-hour work week. They share with the young a repugnance for competitive endeavor, for established definitions of success, and for many of the values which "straight" society holds dear.

Today the communal scene is made up of groups which differ from each other as radically as those of the previous century. Urban communes are often simple rent-sharing arrangements, but they may also be made up of people who live together because of their interest in a cause in which they are jointly engaged—rock music, religion, service to others, group sex, the publication of a newspaper. The rural utopian communes come in every size, shape, and persuasion. Some are highly organized groups of disciplined hard-working people with an indomitable sense of commitment. Others are gypsy encampments where vagrant idlers crash for a while and move on. Some groups run successful farms, others practice crafts, some run small industries, some have fashioned squalid rural slums and others tidy little enclaves. There are political activist communes, homosexual communes, at least three Black Muslim communes. There are ever-increasing numbers of religious communes, although the religion practiced may be Christianity, Buddhism, Pantheism, or something one of the members made up from bits and ends and snatches. There are several Quaker communes. Thousands of young people, in their search for new values, are turning to an ecstatic form of Christianity which, in many ways, is reminiscent of the old-time revivalism. Mass baptisms are conducted in the surf at California beaches; instant conversions are celebrated with fervor. Among the so-called Jesus people self-knowledge through religion is perhaps more emphasized than salvation or good works, although many groups go out into the community to help sufferers, particularly drug addicts. Considerable attention has recently been directed toward a radical sect of the Jesus people known as the Children of God, who preach that the world will end in about twenty years. Many of these young men and women are former drug users who have found peace and joy in their ascetic life. They dress in red sackcloth, eschew drugs, tobacco, and alcohol, spend their days in hymn singing and Bible study, devoting themselves "100 percent to the Lord." It is estimated that they now have two thousand members in forty communes.

Journalist Robert Houriet, who spent a year visiting fifty communes, objects to the stereotype of communitarians as people primarily interested in drugs and sex. These commodities are too available in the outside world to serve as a cause which can hold people together, he points out. Although he met many *former* heavy drug users, he saw no one on a commune who was on speed or heroin. As to sex, Houriet says, "It's largely monogamous . . . not nearly as orgiastic as people think."

What is now regarded as the first rural hippie commune opened in the distant dark ages of 1966, when a middle-aged former jazz musician named Lou Gottlieb threw open the gates of Morningstar, his California ranch, and invited any and all to encamp. Hundreds came and made their nests in tents, tepees, shacks, tree houses. Some simply tossed old mattresses on the ground. When the county authorities attempted to close the project down because of its total lack of running water or any sanitary facilities, Gottlieb—in the grand tradition of flamboyant eccentrics—turned over the deed to the property to God and declared it "open land." When he signed the contract he paid a dollar, to make it official.

Most of the early residents of Morningstar moved on years ago but a few remain and newcomers trickle in. Morningstar's do-your-own-thing gypsies never formed a group which could in any way be called a community, although considerable sharing prevailed. The place does, however, have a written official "faith" and a list of taboos. Among the forbidden acts are: hurting others, exploiting the elements, planning ahead, living luxuriously, breathing polluted air, checking natural urges.

Many of the drifters who shambled away from Morningstar recamped ten miles down the road, where Wheeler Ranch was also opened to the young in 1967. Newcomers fashioned shelters in abandoned autos, tents, and caves, and a few outhouses were installed and some vegetable gardens started by more practical members. The casual nudity of many of the hoers and pickers caused considerable displeasure in the nearby communities, as did the presumed sexual promiscuity.

The desire to "groove with nature" caught on like a contagion. Morningstar East was started north of Taos, New Mexico—which was to become the most heavily populated hip-commune area of the country. In southern California a group calling itself the Hog Farm set off in psychedelically painted buses to become a commune-on-wheels after a year of surviving by plucking food from restaurant and grocery store trash cans. Among the hills and mesas of New Mexico new families were rapidly springing into being. At New Buffalo, city-born kids erected tepees and began to farm their acreage, which had been purchased for fifty thousand dollars by a wealthy member. Any wanderer looking for a place to squat and be idle was informed that the community was busy making adobe bricks, and that if this wasn't his thing he'd better see about *making* it his thing if he wanted to live there. Other communes were started in the area. The members of Lorien—named for Tolkien's Land of the Elves—determined, like the New Buffaloans, to work constructively and to seek peaceable relations with the neighbors. As is the case with most hip communes, their property was bought by an affluent member—in this case a drop-out Philadelphia poet who cashed in his IBM stock.

All over the West, boys whose fathers worked in air-conditioned twenty-story office buildings were discovering how to grow wheat, and girls whose mothers never dreamed of making bread were finding mystical joy in learning to knead and to bake. They were also learning to build. In two Colorado communes, Drop City and Libre, shelters based on the design of a geodesic dome were being constructed; metal roofs cut from discarded cars were sawed, shaped, and set into wooden frames. The urban, college-bred residents of Big Foot, a well-organized community in Mendocino County, California, built a twenty-five-by-fifty-foot communal house which was passed on all counts by a dubious building inspector. They also built individual "sleeping houses" for members, each one out of sight of the others. Few communities offer this sort of privacy.

Big Foot, like so many other communes, was originally financed by one member. The members have been reasonably successful with various farm projects—goats, chickens, bees, and vegetable gardening—and they barter some of their produce for needed food with other farmers in the area and with fishing crews. Also, several members go out to work on jobs outside the community for added income. This is the practice at many of the more stable communes. A Drop City and Libre, where there are a number of artist members, sale of paintings and sculpture helps pad the budget. At many communes most members still receive financial assistance from home. Many communitarians apply for the Federal food stamp program and collect welfare payments—although in some communes this practice is scorned. The feeling that society owes financial support to its drop-outs is becoming less prevalent, and in the more stable communes such aid is now usually considered acceptable only as an emergency measure. Panhandling occurs in some places and is unheard of in others. The sale of hand-made craft items and farm produce is a common source of money.

Almost all contemporary communes—like those of the past—have encountered hostility from "straight" society. After the Manson Family murders, a building in Taos displayed a painted sign saying: THE ONLY GOOD HIPPIE IS A DEAD HIPPIE. KILL. Manson referred to his band of followers, most of them tragically alienated young girls, as his "Family." Like many communalists he had established his household in the desert—in his case an old movie set ranch—after a brief stint in Haight-Ashbury. Here the resemblance between the peace-loving, predominantly middle-class hippies and Charles Manson, the severely disturbed illegitimate child of a prostitute, ceased. When he was tried for the murder of film star Sharon Tate and six other persons Manson had already spent thirteen years in reform schools and penitentiaries as the result of a varied and brutal career in crime.

Although rural communalists have proven to be extraordinarily peaceable folk, they have been verbally linked with violent "bikers" and psychopathic murderers by people who are outraged by their casual attitudes toward marijuana, sex, and nudity, and who view them as a threat to the morals of local teen-agers. People who would be dismayed to hear that Mother Ann Lee was beaten for her beliefs have been known to consider it fair game to shoot into communal settlements from automobiles and set fire to barns.

More commonly, the protest has been nonviolent. The squalor of many communes and frequent cases of hepatitis have offered townsfolk legal opportunities for action. "Most communes can be closed down by health regulations if someone wants to enough," says a woman from Heathcote, a commune in Pennsylvania which publishes a journal of the movement, *The Green Revolution.*

Heathcote has been notably successful in its community relations, but another Pennsylvania commune, the Land of Oz, has become a frequently discussed case history in the annals of failure. Located near Meadville, Pennsylvania, on a farm inherited by one of its members, this assorted group of flower children, aged sixteen through forty-two, sought converts and found a good many takers among the teenagers in nearby towns. Local merchants refused to sell to them; they were threatened and harassed; a dog on the commune was shot; a girl was attacked, and a charge was brought against them of "maintaining a disorderly house." They were told that the charge would be dropped if they moved within two weeks and the commune disbanded.

Oz lasted four months, and an unknown number of other communes have gone through the same brief life cycle for similar reasons. Some have been destroyed by external pressures and many others by internal discord. Those with no structure or leadership are doomed from the start. Excessive numbers of visitors have caused the collapse of some communities, and most of the well-organized groups now have definite rules and visitors' fees to avoid this problem. Some communities actively seek members —particularly those who can make a financial contribution—and others have firmly closed down membership.

Structure, stability, and carefully guarded peaceful neighborhood relations exist at Twin Oaks, fifty miles from Richmond, Virginia, where a group of about twenty-five adults has set up a community based on B. F. Skinner's utopian novel *Walden II*. Prospective members must work during a probationary period of several months before acceptance. To achieve membership they must then pay an entrance fee of two hundred dollars. Visitors are required to make advance arrangements, pay for their food, obey certain rules, and work during their stay, as did the visitors in *Walden II*. Like its model, Twin Oaks has planners and managers; jobs are chosen by labor credits; many members wear plastic counters to register their own bad habits which they attempt to change by "self-management." The counters may be automatic types worn on the wrist or at the belt, or they may be beads. People wearing them keep track of their own undesirable actions and become more aware of habits they hope to break. Desirable habits are also tallied and "reinforced" by a system of rewards. In this tidy, conventionally dressed, and orderly group, drugs and alcohol are forbidden, as are idleness and gossip. Unlike Walden II, where members work only four hours a day and child rearing is a major issue, members of Twin Oaks average six hours' work daily and must also rotate working outside the community to bring in income. Childbearing is being postponed until the community is on a firmer financial footing. Work credits are earned by selecting jobs from a list of needed chores, and although a definite *amount* of work is required, jobs can be done at any hour of the day or night that is preferred. The community prints a newsletter, uses any labor-saving machines it is able to acquire, and runs a successful hammock-making business. Meetings for mutual criticism are held in a community building named—Oneida! The hammock-making takes place in a large shelter named Harmony.

The fictional Walden II had certain advantages over Twin Oaks. It had been blessed with a million-dollar donation and had a population of one thousand members. Twin Oaks is a long way from the idyllic total self-sufficiency of Walden II. Nonetheless, it continues to uphold behaviorist principles and to imitate Walden II's detailed conventions. No personal titles whatsoever are used, private rooms are provided, many individual preferences are sacrificed for practical reasons. Twin Oaks may be the only commune which buys ordinary commercial white bread—because the members find it cheaper than making their own.

The residents of Twin Oaks are very positive about their goals and ideals, but this makes them an exception to the majority of today's commune-dwellers. A questionnaire which asked whether settlements had a specific set of commitments resulted in the information that most did not subscribe to a *particular* movement, but felt themselves allied to "the Movement." What is indicated is a fuzzy general approval of beliefs in conservation, peace, nonviolence, new Leftism, communal rearing of children, natural childbirth, mysticism, sexual freedom, nudism, "soft" drugs, encounter-group therapy, rural living, natural diet, old-time crafts.

To many of these new pioneers, the direct gratification of learning to make useful things, to grow edible food, and to survive without the comforts of "civilization" is exhilaratingly enriching and sustaining. To others—brought up in middle-class security—the privations and demands of the new life are totally devastating. Today's communitarians are, in almost every case, consciously lowering their standard of living, which was not the case in the nineteenth century. Most of the stable communes of the past offered struggling farmers and industrial workers a life that was more secure, more healthy, and more comfortable than that available in the outside world. They extended equality and dignity to women and permitted an existence eased by shared responsibilities and companionship. Children were given better than average education in many cases and all were taught agricultural skills and trades. Today's young people, fleeing unhappy situations at home and at school, often find themselves even more discontented in the demanding atmosphere of the commune. Professor Skinner believes that most communes fail "because of the desire for immediate ecstasy" on the part of the underdisciplined and overpampered. The simple life—complete with poor food, inadequate shelter, and total lack of privacy— sounds like fun to many adventurers who soon find it intolerable. Casual sexual relations can prove destructive, and submerging individuality to the group interest when it becomes important is often impossible for people insufficiently imbued with the long view.

And yet for many people today communal life is not just an intensely satisfying experience in meaningful human relationships, but has become the *only* acceptable way of life. The effort of many totally committed communitarians is reflected in increasing numbers of stable—even prosperous—communes. Attitudes which work *against* rather than *for* success are being discarded, and many groups now view friendly relations with the "straight" world, careful screening of new candidates for admission, and planning and budgeting as necessities for survival. Conferences are being held at which communitarians exchange ideas on bartering, cooperative buying at wholesale rates, and matters which can only be described as "business management." The Brotherhood of the Spirit, whose 250 members live in Massachusetts, work on construction jobs and on farms and have an experienced financial manager and systems analyst handling their monetary affairs. Certainly community is going to become a permanent lifestyle for a great many contemporary Americans as it was for thousands of men and women of the previous century.

Of course, whether or not the success of communal settlements can be judged primarily by their longevity is yet another question. Brook Farm, with a life span of six years, was the only major nineteenth-century community to end with harmonious relations between its members. Along with a number of other secular communes of short duration the experiment generated new and liberal ideas on education, gave impetus to movements for the abolition of slavery, for women's rights, and for improved working and living conditions for the poor. The long-lived insular religious communities provided a good life for their members but had little impact on the outside world. Many of today's communitarians use the word "success" to refer only to the effect of the communal experience on the individual. Others view cooperative living as a demonstration to the outside world of a life that is more spiritually valid, more creative, more loving, and more humane.

Utopia—the land that cannot be found on any map of

the world—continues to excite the imagination of dreamers and explorers. Man is good but society is evil, today's utopians are saying, as utopians have said through the ages. If man discovers an ideal society in which to live he can shake off faulty social teachings and the corruption of today's world, say the new utopians—as did the old. Can man free himself of the shackles of class and materialism and the sins of competitive ruthlessness and greed? Can man—in short—achieve perfection in a new world of his own devising? Yes, cry the new utopians, as did their forebears. Yes. Yes. Yes.

# About the Author

Elinor Horwitz was born in New Haven, Connecticut, and was graduated from Smith College. Her marriage to neurosurgeon Norman Horwitz brought her to Chevy Chase, Maryland, where they live with their three children. The Horwitzes are avid collectors of books, Persian miniatures, and Islamic pottery.

Professionally, Elinor Horwitz has written for many major national magazines and is a regular feature writer for the *Washington Evening Star*. Her previous books for children are THE STRANGE STORY OF THE FROG WHO BECAME A PRINCE and THE SOOTHSAYER'S HANDBOOK—A GUIDE TO BAD SIGNS AND GOOD VIBRATIONS.